JESUS AND THE PLEASURES

J. Christian Wilson

MINNEAPOLIS

JESUS AND THE PLEASURES

Large-quantity purchases or custom editions of this book are available at a discount from the publisher. For more information, contact the sales department at Augsburg Fortress, Publishers, 1-800-328-4648, or write to: Sales Director, Augsburg Fortress, Publishers, P.O. Box 1209, Minneapolis, MN 55440-1209.

ISBN 0-8066-3464-2

Cover design by Brad Norr Design; Cover art by Charles Perkalis
Book design by Michelle L. N. Cook

The paper used in this publication meets the minimum requirements of American National Standard for Information Sciences—Permanence of Paper for Printed Library Materials, ANSI Z329.48-1984. ♾ ™

Manufactured in the U.S.A.

07 06 05 04 03 1 2 3 4 5 6 7 8 9 10

To Marianne

for the pleasure of her company

CONTENTS

1 / THE PLEASURES

"WHO DOES NOT LOVE WINE, WOMEN, AND SONG,
REMAINS A FOOL HIS WHOLE LIFE LONG."
—JOHANN HEINRICH VOSS

It is not the normal quotation with which one would expect a book about Jesus to begin. Throughout the centuries the Christian Church has been much more inclined to portray Jesus as a model monk, a neutered nerd who stood above the cares and concerns, wants and desires of normal human beings, and certainly not a lover of the pleasures of this life, certainly not one to love wine, women, and song.

The Church's Jesus brought blessing and healing to the poor and the sick. He sternly rebuked those who opposed the way of God. But he had virtually nothing in the way of personal feelings himself. He loved people but never longed to be loved. He healed people but felt no hurts himself, except for perhaps a few moments on the cross.

The contention of this book is that the barely human Jesus of the Church's history is not the Jesus of the Gospels. The Jesus of the Gospels rejected the ascetic, pleasure-denying ways of many of his contemporaries such as the Essenes, who wrote the Dead Sea Scrolls, and John the Baptist. However much Jesus may have respected them and honored them for their faithfulness to God, their ways were not his ways. Jesus brought a new way, the way that leads to life—not just pie-in-the-sky-by-and-by life eternal, but new life in the here and now. Jesus leads us to the joy of the good life. He helps us to find in ourselves and all that surrounds us the pleasures of the good things.

JESUS WAS A MAN

Whatever else Jesus may have been, he was a human being. The writings of the New Testament make this clear again and again: "And the Word became flesh and lived among us, and we have seen his glory, the glory as of the father's only son, full of grace and truth" (John 1:14). "Every spirit that confesses that Jesus Christ has come in the flesh is from God" (1 John 4:2). Yet the Christian Church over the centuries has tended to maximize the divinity of Jesus and minimize his humanity. The Nicene Creed, written in the fourth century C.E., calls Jesus "God from God, Light from Light, true God from true God, begotten not made, of one Being with the Father," but says next to nothing about his humanity. Yet, for all its efforts to dehumanize Jesus, the Church does not quite want to abolish his humanity altogether.

One group of early Christians did want to abolish Jesus' humanity. They were called the Gnostics, a word that comes from the Greek word for "knowledge." The Gnostics claimed to have secret knowledge about Jesus, God, and all the spirits of the universe. They believed that the entire created realm, indeed anything of material substance, was evil. Humans, the most fleshly and material of creatures, were irretrievably evil in their bodies. Only that one nonmaterial part of them, their soul, was good. Because all things material were evil, and because the human body was material, or so they believed, Jesus must not have had a human body. For if he did, he would have had to be evil.

The Christian Church soon recognized Gnosticism to be heresy, that is, too far from the Christian mainstream to be acceptable. By the late second century, the Christian Church father Irenaeus of Lyon wrote extensively against the Gnostics, explaining and denouncing their flesh-denying doctrine.

By the fifth century C.E., Gnosticism was virtually gone. Yet the gnostic *tendency* has remained. Although the Church never wants to deny the humanity of Jesus completely, it certainly does not want to emphasize it. The Jesus of Christianity is, in the words of theologian Ernst Käsemann, "God astride the earth," a spiritual being, human only in his chemical composition.

This quasi gnostic view pervades evangelical and fundamentalist Christianity, the most prominent forms of the religion in America at present. It also utterly misses the point.

The point is that God became flesh. The Church consistently fails to embrace fully the ancient doctrine of the incarnation, that God came to earth "in-carnate." That's Latin for literally "in the meat." The Church can accept the doctrine of the incarnation in so far as it means that Jesus was not a disembodied spirit but had a human body. The Church does not seem to want the full doctrine of the incarnation. It does not want Jesus to be fully human, to have human feelings, emotions, and desires, to enjoy the fully human pleasures of this life.

The saddest part of this denial is that when we deny the full humanity of Jesus, we also deny our own full humanity. When we deny that Jesus fully participated in the pleasures of this life, we deny the possibility of our own full enjoyment of those pleasures.

This book celebrates the humanity of Jesus. The credo of this book is that Jesus is "man of man, true man of true man." The mystery and power of the incarnation—the belief that sets Christianity apart from all other religions—is that God became a human being in Jesus of Nazareth.

The present-day gnosticized forms of Christianity seek for the human spirit to be free from the pleasures of the flesh. God, who was pure divine spirit, sought just the opposite. God sought to become human—and God accomplished what God sought. God became a flesh-and-blood human being at a particular place in the world and at a particular time in history. That human being lived one particular human life on this earth, and that particular human died a tragically human death.

The biggest trend in Christianity today is a spirituality in which Jesus shows us the way to God. It is not just conservative evangelicals and fundamentalists who are riding the crest of this trend. Christian liberals and moderates also are seeking "spiritual formation." Catholics and mainline denominational Protestants are having spirituality seminars and going on spiritual life retreats. Their priests and preachers are continually telling us how "spiritually hungry" we are and continually creating new ways for that hunger to be filled.

The emphasis of the New Testament Gospels, however, is that Jesus shows us the way to ourselves. Jesus did not come just to make us more spiritual. Even more importantly, he came to show us the way to be more fully human. The emphasis of Christianity not only dehumanizes Jesus, it dehumanizes humanity as well. It teaches us to value our spirits above our bodies, to see the pleasures of this life as sins to be avoided, and to make us believe that we should become more like God.

THE FIRST SIN

God does not want us to become more like God. This is the point of the ancient story of Adam and Eve. In it God creates prototypical humans to live and breathe in human flesh. God puts them in a paradisical garden of delights, with the intention that they live in a wealth of earthly pleasure. They were meant to live in harmony with nature and each other, enjoying all the pleasures that life could afford.

Many myths and misunderstandings have grown up around the story of Adam and Eve. One misunderstanding is that life in paradise was static, changeless. Another is that Adam and Eve were confined to the garden. In the story the garden was their home—it was not their limit. The garden became closed only after they were expelled from it. Before the fall they were free to travel wherever they wished.

Another misunderstanding of the story is the idea that before the fall Adam and Eve did not work, that work was a punishment for sin. Yet the story makes it quite clear that before the fall, "The LORD God took the man and put him in the garden of Eden to till it and keep it" (Gen. 2:15). Still another misunderstanding is that they would be celibate and childless. Nothing in the story suggests this. That most fleshly of human pleasures, human sexuality, was created in them for their enjoyment. The story assumes that Adam and Eve's intercourse would lead to childbearing, and that childbearing would lead to the populating of the earth. Eve's punishment after the fall is not childbearing but increased pain in childbearing (Gen. 3:16).

Christians throughout the ages have often seen sex as the sin of Adam and Eve. Yet sex is not even mentioned in the story of their fall. Other Christians have seen any kind of disobedience to God as the sin of Adam and Eve. In this instance it was disobedience regarding a matter as trivial as eating fruit. This is not the point of the story either. The point of the story, the real sin of Adam and Eve, is that they wanted not to be the humans they were created to be, but to be

God. When the serpent tempts Eve with the fruit of the tree of knowledge of good and evil, she responds that God has forbidden her to eat from that tree. The serpent then tells her that if she eats of the forbidden tree, she "will be like God" (Gen. 3:5). God had created her to be human. God had created her in the flesh. God had given to Adam and her all they needed for the goodness of life. They could be disobedient to God in only one way. That one way was to try to deny their humanity and become like God.

Ironically, this legendary first human sin is the major sin of Christians today and throughout the last two millennia. This present-day sin is grounded in the belief that humans are inherently evil. It is the doctrine called "original sin." The doctrine is never stated in the Bible itself; it was formulated four centuries after the life of Jesus by St. Augustine (354–430 C.E.). The doctrine is based primarily on one passage from Psalm 51 and an interpretation of St. Paul's interpretation of the Old Testament and the meaning of Christ.

> For I know my transgressions,
> and my sin is ever before me.
> Against you, you alone, have I sinned,
> and done what is evil in your sight,
> so that you are justified in your sentence
> and blameless when you pass judgment.
> Indeed, I was born guilty,
> a sinner when my mother conceived me.
> (Ps. 51:3–5)

While Christianity has long understood the statements in this psalm to be applicable to all human beings, the superscription of the psalm puts it in a single historical setting: "To the leader. A Psalm of David, when the prophet Nathan came to him, after he had gone in to Bathsheba."

David had been involved in an extramarital affair with Bathsheba while her husband, Uriah the Hittite, had been away from home, fighting the wars as a loyal soldier in King David's army. Bathsheba became pregnant during the affair. David contrived a plan to bring Uriah home for a few days so that everyone would think that Uriah and Bathsheba conceived the baby during that time. But Uriah refused to go down to his house; instead he slept on David's doorstep, saying (in accordance with the customs of ancient warfare) that he could not sleep with his wife as long as his comrades were in combat.

David then had to contrive a plan B. Plan B was much more vicious than plan A had been. David summoned his general Joab and told him to put Uriah at the front line of the next battle. Joab was to give a special retreat signal that everyone but Uriah would know. Then all the troops would retreat, leaving Uriah surrounded by the enemy. The plan worked, and Uriah was killed. David then married his widow, Bathsheba, thinking that he had gotten away with the affair. He should have known better. High public officials hardly ever succeed at keeping extramarital affairs secret. Nathan the prophet came to David and told him a story:

There was a rich man and a poor man. The rich man had vast flocks, but the poor man had only one little lamb, which he dearly loved. One day the rich man had a guest come for dinner. Instead of cooking a lamb from his own vast flock, the rich man took the poor man's lamb and used it for the dinner.

David became quite angry when he heard the story. He burst out saying, "As the LORD lives, this man who has done this deserves to die; he shall restore the lamb fourfold, because he did this thing, and because he had no pity" (2 Sam. 12:5–6). Nathan then looked David straight in the eye and said, "You are the man," and launched into a full condemnation of what David had done, replete with a list of punishments from God that David would suffer. The whole story is told in the Second Book of Samuel, chapters 11–12.

Although Psalm 51 was probably not written by David himself, the psalm is clearly set in the specific situation of the story of David and Bathsheba. Should the words of the psalm be applied not just to David but to all people? And even if they are to be applied to all people, what do they mean?

The Church has traditionally gone with a different translation of the last line in Psalm 51:5, such as that in the King James Version: "In sin did my mother conceive me." The Church has understood this to mean that the act by which conception occurs, namely sexual intercourse, is sinful. Of course this is not what the Hebrew text of the Psalm actually says. The New Revised Standard Version is much closer to the Hebrew. Nowhere in the Hebrew Bible does it say that sin is passed like a gene from one generation to the next. Nowhere in the Bible does it say that sexual intercourse is sinful.

Augustine's other major source for his doctrine of original sin was St. Paul. In his letter to the Romans, Paul says the following:

> Therefore, just as sin came into the world through one man, and death came through sin, and so death spread to all because all have sinned—sin was indeed in the world before the law, but sin is not reckoned when there is no law. Yet death exercised dominion from Adam to Moses, even over those whose sins were not like the transgression of Adam, who is a type of the one who was to come. (Rom. 5:12–14)

The Church, beginning with Augustine, deduced from this passage that the sin of Adam has been passed down to all people. It is a point worth being picky about. That is not what Paul says. What Paul says is that Adam's death was the result of Adam's sin, and that death spread from Adam to all people (even Jesus). Because all have sinned, all are deserving of the death they receive. Paul does *not* say that sin is inherited. Moreover, Paul makes it clear that sin and death do not have dominion over humanity because Christ has shattered the power of sin and death. Paul writes:

> For the judgment following one trespass brought condemnation, but the free gift following many trespasses brings justification. If, because of the one man's trespass, death exercised dominion through that one, much more surely will those who receive the abundance of grace and the free gift of righteousness exercise dominion in life through the one man, Jesus Christ. (Rom. 5:16–17)

Whatever power sin may have had is nullified through the life, death, and resurrection of Jesus Christ. Christ frees human beings to follow their true nature, which is not sinful but good. The truly human Jesus shows us our humanity.

JESUS AND OUR HUMANITY

This book is concerned with a few aspects of our lives as human beings. It is not a life guide, a blueprint for how one should live life. It is not a guide for getting through difficult times in our lives, it is not concerned with many of the larger issues of Christian theology, and it does not provide guidelines for government and international relations. Rather, it is a book about some of the simple pleasures that make life worth living, and about finding life fulfillment in these simple pleasures. It is a book that encourages us to be more fully human. It is based on the life, actions, and words of Jesus of Nazareth, and is filled with scripture references and quotations relating to his life.

The first chapters deal more with Jesus than with us. In these chapters I seek primarily to show how Jesus dealt with the issues of life's pleasures, although I certainly touch on how what Jesus said and did relates to us. In the last chapter, I hope to show how we twenty-first-century Americans, in our pursuit of a life of goodness, happiness, and pleasure, can find Jesus in our midst.

2 / SIMPLE PLEASURES IN THE GALILEE

Jesus was not a monk. Jesus was a man of pleasure, a lover of the pleasures of this life. He taught a philosophy of pleasure that is extraordinary in its simplicity, yet profound in its depth. Jesus left no writings. What we know of his thought, we know only indirectly—through the writings of followers of his followers, who wrote a full generation after his death. During the century in which he lived, four of these writers penned their spiritual biographies of him, biographies that from earliest times have been called Gospels.

The Gospels achieved renown within a century of their writing, and would become a part of the Christian Bible. A fifth account, the Gospel of Thomas, would be taken up by a group that the Christians branded as heretics. When this group died out over the course of the late fourth and early fifth centuries, the reading and copying of the Gospel of Thomas died out with them. Only in 1945 would a complete copy of this valuable source of Jesus' teachings be rediscovered, quite accidentally, by a local farmer in northern Egypt.

The five Gospels do not begin to tell all that Jesus did and taught. They provide no information about his life between the ages of twelve and thirty. But they do provide extensive information about the last three years of his thirty-three-year life. These teachings reveal the thought of a great man, a deeply caring and loving man, whose life was tragically cut short by those who neither cared nor loved. The dramatic and horrible circumstances of his death, along with the perception among his followers that he had risen from the dead, created a movement that would evolve into one of the world's great religions. Perhaps it is unfortunate that his death and resurrection have long relegated his teachings to a subordinate place in Christianity's understanding of him. From the time of the earliest Christian writer, Paul of Tarsus, Jesus' death has been far more important than his life. His death has been conceived as the central and decisive act in a divine plan of history. In this scenario his life is a mere prelude, a demonstration through his miracle-working, of his divinity.

This book seeks to elevate the importance of the life of Jesus, especially the part of his life that can be of renewed significance for us today, his teachings. One might think that his teachings have been studied to death by now. Certainly no other person's thought in all of human history has borne as much scrutiny, and no other person's thought has had as much written about it. Can there possibly be anything new to say?

Recent scholarly writing on Jesus has gone in two remarkably different directions. One group of scholars sees Jesus as a fire-breathing prophet of doom who foresaw and warned of the imminent judgment of God leading to the destruction of the world. Of course the world was not destroyed. This group, whose ideas go back to the great scholar and humanitarian Albert Schweitzer in the early twentieth century, concludes that Jesus was wrong at the most central point in his message.

Another group of more recent vintage regards Jesus as somewhat of a cynic-stoic itinerant philosopher, an early hippie who preached a life of freedom from possessions and family ties, of peace and love and a lack of responsibility. His message was antiestablishment, antiwealth, antimaterialism, and antigovernment. Though not a violent revolutionary, he was something of an anarchist.

Of course the vast majority of people who have some acquaintance with the teachings of Jesus fall into neither of these camps. They see Jesus as their Churches have taught them to see Jesus: as a pious holy man who taught a strict code of ethical behavior. They believe that this code emphasizes practices of self-denial and abstinence that ensure eternal life in heaven and avoidance of eternal damnation and pain in hell. They see themselves as unable fully to live up to the teachings of Jesus. They feel some guilt about this, but they also live with some assurance of God's forgiveness and grace, which will get them to heaven when their own deeds will not.

In past years, through my grandmother's lifetime and well into the twentieth century, many people lived with a genuine fear of going to hell. Now no one is afraid of going to hell. To be sure, many people believe that others will go to hell, but they see no possibility of such damnation for themselves, sinners though they may be.

This book offers something of a fresh look at the authentic teachings of Jesus. These teachings portray a man who was neither a prophet of doom, a prototypical hippie, nor a model monk. Jesus was a man of pleasure. He understood and appreciated the pleasures of this life, and he sought to bring a life of deeper and truer pleasure to everyone he encountered, not just the rich, not just the holy, not just the healthy.

A PLACE OF HUMAN-MADE BEAUTY

Jesus grew up in circumstances that by the standards of twenty-first-century America would be considered poverty, though they were quite normal and average for his own time and place. The pleasures of his life were not the pleasures afforded by wealth; he found his pleasures in other things.

Jesus learned of the ordinary pleasures of life that we all, or almost all, experience from infancy. He knew the love of his mother. He knew the satisfaction of bodily nourishment, of physical and social contact with people close to him, of a good night's sleep.

Jesus also knew another pleasure that not all of us experience. He grew up in close proximity to places of great beauty. The region of lower Galilee, where his home village of Nazareth was located, is in a lush, green valley surrounded by lovely hills. Nazareth was not much, just a stop on the road, but it was near two places of great beauty, one natural and one made by human hands. A mere three miles from Nazareth was the magnificent Greco-Roman city of Sepphoris. We knew little of Sepphoris until archaeologists excavated it in the late 1980s. What they found was a city of elegant and finely crafted classical architecture. In one of its buildings they uncovered a mosaic of a young woman. The mosaic is of such extraordinary beauty that it has been dubbed the "Mona Lisa of the Galilee."

Sepphoris was under construction during Jesus' lifetime. Although the Gospels tell us nothing about Jesus from the time he was twelve until he was thirty, they do tell us that his occupation was *tekton*, a Greek word (all the Gospels were originally written in Greek) that is usually translated "carpenter." When we think of the word *carpenter*, we think of someone who works with hammer, nails, and wood. But Galilee, now and at the time of Jesus, has few trees and little wood. Houses and buildings are built primarily of stone. Jesus was more likely a stonemason than what we would call a carpenter.

Where would he have worked? Probably not in Nazareth, where little in the way of building was going on at this time. He could have gone to Jerusalem and worked on the Temple, which was in the process of reconstruction during his entire lifetime. But Jerusalem was a considerable distance from this home. Sepphoris was less than an hour's walk. It certainly seems possible, if not probable, that the young Jesus found work in Sepphoris. Could he even have been one of the mosaic artists who created the "Mona Lisa of the Galilee"?

Though I have never been a builder, I have known many. All of them take pleasure in the work of their hands and see beauty in the things they have made. They find satisfaction in their work. It surely must have been satisfying for Jesus to see the works of his hands. It must have been satisfying for him to see the building of Sepphoris. But at age thirty he would go into a different line of work in a different place. The crafter of stone would become a crafter of words and thoughts.

A PLACE OF SIMPLE PLEASURE

During his thirtieth year, Jesus was baptized in the Jordan River, just south of the Sea of Galilee. At his baptism he felt a calling to a different life in a different place. He would no longer be a *tekton*, but would become a teacher. He would be called by the Hebrew word for teacher, *rabbi*. He would leave his family in Nazareth to live and teach around the Sea of Galilee. On those few occasions when he would return to Nazareth as a teacher, he would find a cool reception:

> He . . . came to his hometown, and his disciples followed him. On the sabbath he began to teach in the synagogue, and many who heard him were astounded. They said, "Where did this man get all this? What is the wisdom that has been given to him? What deeds of power are being done by his hands! Is not this the carpenter [tekton], the son of Mary and brother of James and Joses and Judas and Simon, and are not his sisters here with us?" And they took offense at him.

Then Jesus said to them, "Prophets are not without honor, except in their hometown, and among their own kin, and in their own house" (Mark 6:1–4).

Those in his hometown knew him too well, or at least so they thought. It was difficult for them to accept that his teaching had any authority for them, because they had known him since he was a little boy. Around the Sea of Galilee he would find a more receptive audience.

The first time I visited the Sea of Galilee was in 1988. I was immediately struck with the natural beauty of the place. Even though it was January, flowers bloomed and the hillsides were green. Beautiful bougainvillea blossoms sprouted from the vines on the buildings in Capernaum, the town where Jesus would spend most of his time. The steep hills around the Sea of Galilee peak at sea level; the Sea of Galilee itself is 650 feet below sea level. The climate of the surrounding shore where Jesus spent most of his ministry is thus very mild in winter and quite hot in summer.

The Sea of Galilee is not a sea, but a freshwater lake, and is often called Lake Tiberius. It is fifteen miles long and eight miles wide at its widest point. Water flows into it on the north side from the Jordan River. On a clear day one can see all the way to the Jordan's source, snow-capped Mount Hermon, in Lebanon. Water empties out of it into the continuation of the Jordan River to the south. Although storms can arise on the lake, it is normally as peaceful and placid a body of water as one will ever find.

We went out in a boat from the city of Tiberius on the west side of the lake to Capernaum on the north side. When we approached the middle of the lake, the boat's captain cut the engines and allowed the boat to stop in the still waters. In the couple of minutes that followed, we all kept silent in prayerful contemplation. The water was utterly still, and the silence was complete—something I rarely experience in America. In those couple of minutes, as I sat in silence gazing at the beauty of the Galilean hillsides, I experienced a wonderful sense of peace. It was ironic to be feeling utter peace in one of the most strife-torn countries in the world. I thought of how many times Jesus must have gone out on boats with his fishermen disciples; the Gospels record several such occasions. I thought that at some time Jesus probably sat in a fishing boat in this same utter silence, gazing at the same lush, beautiful hillsides in the distance. I could understand for the first time what had to be one of the reasons Jesus picked this place to live. It was a place of rare beauty, a place of simple pleasure. It was a place whose beauty would bring anyone closer to nature—and a place whose silence would bring anyone closer to God.

Jesus, like the other people who lived around the Sea of Galilee, led a simple life. There was scarcely any wealth where he lived. Subsistence farming and fishing were the principal means of living. The Roman government demanded a considerable amount of tax, enough to keep the economy of lower Galilee at a low level, but not enough to cause dire poverty or provoke revolution.

Revolution would come in Galilee thirty-six years after the life of Jesus. The Roman occupying army had already been in Galilee since 63 B.C.E. Roman occupation forces were a part of daily life. Jesus was a Galilean Jew. His people had relatively little to do with the Romans, though Jesus would show a more open-minded attitude toward the Romans than would most of his fellow Galileans.

From the Roman point of view, Galilee was considered an insignificant backwater of the Roman Empire. The population was fairly sparse. Insignificant wealth and commerce, coupled with a lack of political unrest, rendered Galilee little Roman attention. Judea and its major city, Jerusalem, demanded much more Roman concern and a much larger occupying military force. There was political unrest among the Judean Jews. Indeed, it would be in Judea, and in Jerusalem specifically, that Jesus would get into difficulty with the Roman authorities, be condemned by the Roman governor, and be executed by Roman soldiers.

Construction of the new city of Tiberius, on the southwestern side of the Sea of Galilee, was in its early stages. Roman occupying forces, relatively small in number, were based there. The Gospels do not record that Jesus ever went there. He spent most of his time in Capernaum, a few miles to the north.

The sayings and parables of Jesus preserved for us in the Gospels reflect their Galilean setting. Jesus speaks with metaphors of agriculture, homemaking, and fishing. He uses these metaphors most often when he talks about his favorite subject, the Kingdom of God: "The kingdom of God is as if someone would scatter seed on the ground, and would sleep and rise night and day, and the seed would sprout and grow" (Mark 4:26–27). "The kingdom of heaven is like yeast that a woman took and mixed in with three measures of flour until all of it was leavened" (Matt. 13:33). "The kingdom of heaven is like a net that was thrown into the sea and caught fish of every kind" (Matt. 13:47). Much more rarely does Jesus use metaphors from the building industry, in which he was formerly employed.

One of the few things that virtually all New Testament scholars agree upon is that the central focus of the preaching of Jesus was the Kingdom of God (Matthew normally uses the term "kingdom of heaven" in the same parables and sayings in which Mark and Luke use the term "kingdom of God").

Jesus never lays out a blueprint of the Kingdom of God, but always speaks of it in figurative language in sayings and parables. One of the most striking things about the Kingdom of God parables is their consistent use of metaphors of growth: "The kingdom of God . . . is like a mustard seed, which, when sown upon the ground, is the smallest of all the seeds on earth; yet when it is sown it grows up and becomes the greatest of all shrubs" (Mark 4:30–32).

Where is the Kingdom? When is the Kingdom? The Pharisees, Jesus' principal debating opponents, ask him this:

> Once Jesus was asked by the Pharisees when the kingdom of God was coming, and he answered, "The kingdom of God is not coming with things that can be observed; nor will they say, 'Look, here it is!' or 'There it is!' For, in fact, the kingdom of God is among you" (Luke 17:20).

The Kingdom of God is a present reality in the midst of us on earth. But like the mustard plant, it starts small and is in the process of growing. It started on the Galilean shore with Jesus and his earliest followers, and it has over the centuries spread across the earth. It is still far from complete; it is complete in heaven but incomplete on earth. Jesus taught his followers to pray a prayer that contains the line, "Thy Kingdom come . . . on earth, as it is in heaven." The followers of Jesus are agents of the Kingdom, who help it to grow on earth. Where is the Kingdom? It is on earth, but not complete. When is the Kingdom? It is now, but growing into the future. Moreover, the Kingdom is not readily apparent. It is here, but you won't see it unless you are looking for it. The following dialogue between Jesus and his disciples is recorded in the Gospel of Thomas:

> His disciples said to him, "When will the Kingdom come?" "It will not come by watching [waiting] for it. They will not say, 'Behold, here!' or 'Behold, there!' Rather, the Kingdom of the Father is spread out upon the earth, and people do not see it" (113:1–4).

What is the kingdom? This is the harder question. Most scholars will say that it is the reign of God on earth. But what does this mean? Jesus never gave us a blueprint because he wanted his followers to help in the creation of the Kingdom on earth. He told us something of what the Kingdom was like, but wanted us to fill in the details.

This book contends that the Kingdom of God, like the area around the Sea of Galilee where Jesus chose to live and carry out his message and ministry, is a place of simple pleasures. These pleasures are as simple as good food and drink, good health, good music to hear, good art to see, and most important, good relationships of love and peace among us. The Kingdom is simpler to conceive than it is to bring it to fruition. The following chapters look at how Jesus understood some of these basic pleasures of life in the Kingdom on earth, and offer a few suggestions for how we can help the Kingdom grow.

3 / JESUS AND WINE

Jesus was a lover of wine. The first miracle Jesus performed was turning water into wine, and it was not just a little wine. He turned six huge vats of water into between 120 and 180 gallons of wine for a big wedding feast in the little town of Cana. Virtually every day of his adult life, Jesus enjoyed the dry red wines that came from the vast vineyards throughout his native region of Galilee. Drinking wine was an enjoyable part of his daily life. As the story of the miracle at Cana implies, Jesus appreciated the pleasure of wine. He deeply enjoyed this pleasure, as he did the other pleasures of life. His opponents contrasted him unfavorably with the teetotaling John the Baptist. Jesus quotes his opponents as calling him "a glutton and a drunkard," (Matt. 11:19, Luke 7:34), charges he never denies. And the value Jesus placed on wine is perhaps most apparent in his use of wine at the Last Supper as a symbol for his blood.

WINE IN THE OLD TESTAMENT

To understand the role that the pleasure of drinking wine played in Jesus' life, we need to learn something about the role wine played in Jesus' culture and biblical heritage. First we need to dispel a myth that has circulated among fundamentalist Christians since the rise of the prohibitionist movement in the late 1800s. These fundamentalists, who take a literalistic approach to so much of the Bible, do not want to take the word *wine* literally. They contend that *wine* in the Bible is not really wine but unfermented grape juice, the Welchade of antiquity. The biblical texts themselves show how preposterous this idea is. From the very first mention of wine in the Bible, it is clear that wine is wine. Genesis 9:21 says, in reference to Noah, "He drank some of the wine and became drunk." Noah did not become drunk on unfermented grape juice. The same Hebrew word for wine *(yayin)* that is used here is used for wine throughout the Old Testament. In the New Testament, the Apostle Paul chastises some of the Christians at Corinth because at their celebration of the Lord's Supper they have kept all the wine to themselves and gotten drunk from it (1 Cor. 11:20–21). The wine of this Corinthian communion service was real wine—the Corinthians who were hogging it were not getting drunk from grape juice. The Greek word (Greek was the original language of the New Testament, as Hebrew was the original language of the Old Testament) that Paul uses here *(oinos)* is the same Greek word used for wine throughout the New Testament. So when the biblical writers are talking about wine, they mean wine—not anything else.

FROM NOAH TO MELCHIZEDEK TO LOT

In the Hebrew Scriptures, wine is spoken of quite frequently and almost always positively. It is spoken of negatively only when it is the cause of drunkenness, and not always then.

In the story of Noah, the writers of Genesis want to impress upon the readers the utter antiquity of wine making. After the great flood, Noah and his sons, Shem, Ham, and Japheth, come out of the ark and onto the land (Gen. 9:18). The next thing that we read is that, "Noah, a man of the soil, was the first to plant a vineyard" (9:20). This story accords well with what we know from historical and archaeological sources about the antiquity of wine making. Viticulture and wine making appear to have been a part of all the cultures of Mediterranean and Middle Eastern antiquity from earliest times. The ancient Sumerians, Egyptians, and Babylonians were all wine makers; likewise the

Greeks, Etruscans, and Romans who came after them. Their art frequently portrays people of all social classes drinking wine. Their literature frequently talks about wine as one of the pleasures of life.

The first biblical wine experience did not end well. Noah got so drunk that he passed out naked in his tent. His embarrassed sons covered him. When he regained consciousness, he cursed his grandson Canaan, son of Ham, because Ham had been the one to discover his drunken nakedness. It was a bad scene for everyone involved.

In a few short chapters, the Book of Genesis takes us from Noah's abysmal wine experience to an experience that is nearly sacramental. After Abraham defeats some local chieftains in battle, King Melchizedek of Salem, who is a priest of God Most High, brings out bread and wine and gives Abraham a blessing from God. Abraham responds by giving Melchizedek a tenth of all the spoils of the battle. This is the first biblical reference to the tithe. It is also a precursor to the sacrament of Holy Communion, which Jesus himself will institute. Melchizedek vanishes from the Genesis narrative as quickly as he appeared. His only reappearance in the Old Testament is in Psalm 110:4, which reads, "You are a priest forever according to the order of Melchizedek." The psalm is rather cryptic, but its reverential attitude toward Melchizedek, combined with the wine-related image of Melchizedek in Genesis, indicates the acceptability and value of wine in holy rituals.

The next mention of wine in the Bible is a sorry story indeed. Abraham's nephew Lot is living in a cave with his two daughters. Barrenness was considered the greatest curse that could befall a woman in biblical antiquity. Lot's unnamed daughters, fearing that they would never have an opportunity to meet men by whom they could bear children, got their father drunk with wine on two consecutive nights. On the first night, the older daughter had sexual intercourse with her father; on the second night, the younger daughter. Both became pregnant and bore sons. The chief point the biblical author wants to make in this sordid legend is that the names of the two sons were Moab and Ben-ammi, the ultimate ancestors of the Moabites and Ammonites, two of Israel's perpetual enemies. The text implies that Israel's age-old enemies are as bad as they are because they are ultimately the products of incest. Like Noah's story, this story demonstrates the ageless truth that severe drunkenness leads to severe consequences.

The Mysterious Wine of Judah

In Genesis, chapter 49, we read the last words of Jacob to his twelve sons. The fourth son, Judah, is particularly significant, because all the kings of the Jews and the messiah are to be descendants of Judah. Jacob's words are as follows:

[8]Judah, your brothers shall praise you;
your hand shall be on the neck of your enemies;
your father's sons shall bow down before you.
[9]Judah is a lion's whelp;
from the prey, my son, you have gone up.
He crouches down, he stretches out like a lion,
like a lioness—who dares rouse him up?
[10]The scepter shall not depart from Judah,
nor the ruler's staff from between his feet,
until tribute comes to him;
and the obedience of the peoples is his.
[11]Binding his foal to the vine
and his donkey's colt to the choice vine,
he washes his garments in wine
and his robe in the blood of grapes;
[12]his eyes are darker than wine,
and his teeth whiter than milk.

Some things about this obscure text are easier to grasp than others. From the imagery of verse 9, the lion will become a symbol of the tribe of Judah. Verse 10 will be read by later generations to imply that all the rulers of the Jews will come from the tribe of Judah, which indeed they do. Verses 11 and 12 are much harder to understand.

Several metaphors are at work here, all of which will be echoed in later scriptures, including the Gospels. It will echo in the Old Testament book of Zechariah, when the prophet describes the messiah entering the holy city of Jerusalem "riding on a donkey, on a colt, the foal of a donkey (9:9). Following Zechariah's prophecy, Jesus came into the city on a donkey (Matt. 21:5, John 12:14–15).

The metaphorical association of wine with blood in verse 11 echoes in the Last Supper. Giving thanks over the wine, Jesus says, "This cup . . . is the new covenant in my blood" (Luke 22:20). Jesus is from the tribe of Judah. From the earliest days of Christianity, the Lord's Supper was celebrated with the understanding that the wine represented, and even in some mystical way became, the blood of Christ.

We also read in this verse that Judah will wash his garments in wine. The comparison here would seem to be between wine and water, which would normally be used to wash garments. It is not manifestly clear how we are to understand this metaphor. Perhaps it is that water is a common substance, whereas wine is tastier, richer, more luxurious. If so, this metaphor echoes in the first miracle Jesus performed, turning water into wine at the wedding feast at Cana.

There is also the metaphorical connection, only indirect in Genesis 49:11, between washing and blood. In Revelation 7:14 we read of the white-robed elders, who "have washed their robes and made them white in the blood of the Lamb." The lamb, too, is metaphorical. In Exodus, chapter 13, the angel of death will pass over the houses of the Israelites who have put the blood of a sacrificed lamb on their doorposts. Jews will thenceforth commemorate the festival of Passover. In the New Testament, Paul applies the Passover imagery to Christ crucified: "Our paschal lamb, Christ, has been sacrificed for us. Therefore, let us celebrate the festival" (1 Cor. 5:7–8). When John the Baptist encountered Jesus, he said, "Look, here is the Lamb of God!" (John 1:36).

All of this imagery, which begins with these strange verses from Genesis, chapter 49, eventually becomes associated in one way or another with Jesus. The final two images, that Judah's eyes are darker than wine and his teeth whiter than milk, are ancient metaphors intended to show Judah as a handsome man. His dark eyes convey a sense of mystery. White teeth, though commonplace in our age, were rare in all the ages before toothpaste and dentistry. Few people had white teeth—or all their teeth.

Everything that is said about Judah, the man in this passage, was understood by its earliest readers as applying to Judah the tribe. Many generations later that tribe included David, and many generations later still, Jesus. Both Judah and David are described in the Bible as handsome men and strong warriors. Although Jesus is not described physically in the New Testament, the earliest readers of the Gospels would think of him with the image of David and of Judah. That image is of a handsome man with dark, mysterious eyes.

Psalm 104

The Psalms are Old Testament songs, for the most part hymns to be sung in worship. Though many have superscriptions with attributions to various Old Testament characters, especially David, most biblical scholars think that virtually all of them were written after David's lifetime, during the period of the Babylonian Exile (586–538 B.C.E.), or the postexilic period. They reflect both the religious thinking and the life philosophy of the Hebrew people during that time.

Psalm 104 is superscribed as a hymn of praise to "God the Creator and Provider." In it the psalmist praises God for many different aspects of creation: for sun and moon, light and dark, mountains and valleys, rivers, streams, and seas. Among the many verses through which the psalmist offers praise to God are these two:

You cause the grass to grow for the cattle,
    and plants for people to use,
to bring forth food from the earth,
    and wine to gladden the human heart. (14–15)

This passage characterizes the understanding of wine held by biblical peoples. Because biblical people consumed wine every day with their meals, food and wine are spoken of together. God created grass, essential for the life of cattle, yet inedible to humans. God created plants, essential for the life of humans, which they use to make their food. Food is a God-given essential of life. Wine is not essential; humans do not need it to live. Even though in antiquity, wine was safer to drink than water, because it lacked the impurities that tainted untreated water, humans could still build up immunity and survive on water. Though wine was not essential, it was no less God-given. Whereas food gives both sustenance and pleasure, wine is a gift of God purely for human pleasure, "to gladden the human heart."

An early mistake of one line of Christian thought was the practice of asceticism, or the denial of pleasure because pleasure was thought to be inherently evil. Biblical people never thought this way; the Jews from biblical times to the present have never thought this way; and Jesus certainly never thought this way.

Wine in the Book of Proverbs

The Book of Proverbs is filled with ancient wisdom, consisting for the most part of brief aphorisms that tell us how to get along in life. In numerous passages the book personifies wisdom itself. In these personified wisdom passages, Wisdom is a woman. She is well organized, she prepares carefully, and she knows exactly what to do to get along well in life, to provide both essential nurture and desired enjoyment for all her children. We are her children.

Wisdom has built her house,
    she has hewn her seven pillars.
She has slaughtered her animals, she has mixed her wine,
    she has also set her table.
She has sent out her servant-girls, she calls
from the highest places in the town.
"You that are simple, turn in here!"
To those without sense she says,
"Come, eat of my bread,
    and drink of the wine I have mixed.

Lay aside immaturity, and live,
and walk in the way of insight" (Prov. 9:1–6).

The references to bread and wine in this text are, to be sure, metaphorical. They refer to all the things wisdom makes available to us for living "in the way of insight." That the author of these lines uses bread and wine as symbols of our mental sustenance is telling. If bread and wine are metaphors for our internal sustenance, we can infer that they were chief elements of physical sustenance for biblical peoples. That often-quoted line from another book of wisdom, *Rubaiyat of Omar Khayyam,* reads in a similar vein, "A loaf of bread, a jug of wine, and thou." It is in these simplest pleasures of life that we often find our greatest peace and joy, as Jesus did.

The writer of Proverbs also recognizes the problems associated with excessive wine consumption, and perhaps even the disease of alcoholism:

Do not look at wine when it is red,
 when it sparkles in the cup
 and goes down smoothly.
At the last it bites like a serpent,
 and stings like an adder.
Your eyes will see strange things,
 and your mind utter perverse things.
You will be like one who lies down in the midst of the sea,
 like one who lies on the top of a mast.
"They struck me," you will say, "but I was not hurt;
 they beat me, but I did not feel it.
When shall I awake?
 I will seek another drink" (23:31–35).

A famous bit of non-biblical Greek wisdom advises "moderation in all things." The good wine that can bring such fine and simple pleasure in day-to-day life can become a heartbreaker, a home wrecker, and even a killer when taken to excess, especially the extreme excess of alcoholism.

Finally, the writer tells of another way in which wine was used in his time:

Give strong drink to one who is perishing,
 and wine to those in bitter distress;
let them drink and forget their poverty,
 and remember their misery no more (Prov. 31:6–7).

The author is dealing here with the situation of the terminally ill. In his time alcohol was the only means of pain relief for those who were dying. The author counsels that it should be used for that purpose. Today we have other means of providing pain relief to the terminally ill. Powerful drugs can make our last days reasonably comfortable and provide for meaningful final moments with the people we love. Too often our Puritan ethic has persuaded us that enduring extreme pain is a form of heroism. Even in the recent past, too many terminally ill patients refused treatment on such grounds, and too many doctors were unwilling to prescribe painkilling drugs for those who were dying. The hospice movement, which has shown us how meaningful the dying days can be, has helped to turn public opinion toward wise management of pain relief for those who are dying.

Wine in Ecclesiastes

Another book of wisdom in the Hebrew Scriptures, immediately following the Book of Proverbs in the canonical order, is Ecclesiastes. Despite its English title, it is perhaps the least ecclesiastical book of the Bible. Like other books of wisdom, both within the Bible and beyond, Ecclesiastes sees the simple pleasures of life as providing some of the most meaningful human experiences. The author, called Qoheleth (which means "the preacher"), writes:

> There is nothing better for mortals than to eat and drink, and find enjoyment in their toil. This also, I saw, is from the hand of God; for apart from him who can eat or who can have enjoyment? (2:24–25).

He continues this theme at several other points in the book:

> Moreover, it is God's gift that all should eat and drink and take pleasure in all their toil (3:13).

> This is what I have seen to be good: it is fitting to eat and drink and find enjoyment in all the toil with which one toils under the sun the few days of the life God gives us; for this is our lot. Likewise all to whom God gives wealth and possessions and whom he enables to enjoy them, and to accept their lot and find enjoyment in their toil—this is the gift of God. For they will scarcely brood over the days of their lives, because God keeps them occupied with the joy of their hearts (5:18–20).

So I commend enjoyment, for there is nothing better for people under the sun than to eat, and drink, and enjoy themselves, for this will go with them in their toil through the days of life that God gives them under the sun (8:15).

In the ninth chapter of Ecclesiastes, these observations about the simple pleasures of life take the form of a command for how we should live: "Go, eat your bread with enjoyment, and drink your wine with a merry heart; for God has long ago approved what you do" (v. 7). And in the tenth chapter, Qoheleth writes:

Feasts are made for laughter;
    wine gladdens life,
and money meets every need (v. 19).

When some people first read these words, they can scarcely believe the words are biblical. Our deeply ingrained idea that the Bible preaches a strict code of fun-denying, antimaterialistic moral rectitude is certainly not reflected here. Blessedly, dour Protestant teetotalism is on the wane. Only fundamentalist Baptists and a few smaller fundamentalist sects still hold this utterly unbiblical view. The rapidly growing "nondenominational" fundamentalist churches, which claim no connection with any Christian tradition, feel free to drink.

My entire life has been spent within the United Methodist Church and its predecessor, the Methodist Church, in the conservative South. I can remember the annual temperance sermon that all Methodist ministers in the 1950s seemed compelled to preach. It was never really a temperance sermon—it was a total-abstinence sermon. When I was in a ninth-grade Methodist youth fellowship program, we were all asked to sign a pledge that we would never drink alcohol. Although my parents did not drink, and I had never tasted alcohol, I stubbornly refused to sign the pledge. I think I may have been the only kid who did not sign it. Even then I realized that I did not want to commit myself to a course of denial for my entire lifetime when things might be very different for me later in life.

I remember women from the Women's Christian Temperance Union (WCTU) coming to speak to our Sunday school class. They taught all the girls what appeared to be something of a WCTU mantra, "Lips that touch liquor shall never touch mine." Virtually everyone who had signed the pledge and said the mantra seemed to have forgotten it by the time we went off to college in the mid-sixties.

In college I drank about as much as the average student, which was a whole lot less than it is now. By the time I had gotten to a United Methodist divinity school in the late sixties, many attitudes were changing. Beer was served at the opening picnic welcoming the first-year students.

By the time of my ordination into the United Methodist ministry, in the early seventies, the pledge we had to take was modified from abstinence from alcohol to abstinence from anything that might be harmful to our ministry. Alcohol was included in a list of potentially harmful things. I decided that it would not be harmful to my ministry; I could in good conscience take this pledge.

After three years of divinity school and five years of work on a Ph.D. in biblical studies, I finally left Duke University and went to be a parish minister at a small United Methodist Church in rural Tennessee, near the Alabama border. What followed was two years of continual culture shock, both for the congregation and for me. Although I had never lived anywhere outside the South, within in a week I was squelching rumors that I was from New Jersey. Shoulder-length hair was found on no male head but mine in the rural community of Triune, Tennessee. I had been accustomed to hearing the 160-voice choir of the stately Gothic Duke University Chapel sing Bach and Mozart in Latin every Sunday, and to the congregation singing the grand old Protestant hymns of Charles Wesley and Isaac Watts. Worship was a bit different in Triune; the choir had a country music/gospel twang. The first church event I attended there was a Saturday night "sangin'." About twenty-five people gathered around a piano and sang gospel tunes for four hours. Few of them needed the songbooks that were provided, but I did. In the four hours, they did not sing a single tune that I knew except "Amazing Grace," and they sang that with an extra chorus and a different tune.

Their assumption about alcohol was that you were either a total abstainer or an alcoholic—there was nothing in between. But I had enough other battles to fight without taking on that one. The very first night, I was asked whether I believed in "race mixing." "You mean 'integration'?" I asked. "Yes, race mixing," Mrs. Ferguson said. Saying that I did believe in it did not endear me to that congregation. During the course of the next two years, my hair got shorter and the members got more tolerant. Somehow the grace and love of God can overcome a lot of differences. During the entire two years, however, I did not touch a drop of alcohol.

What a far cry those years are from the present. In the third week of the year 2000, I was invited to a dinner for ordained clergy and their spouses at the parsonage of Christ United Methodist Church in Greensboro, North

Carolina. The senior pastor and his wife served wine with dinner. Only the older retired clergy did not drink it. No one seemed disturbed that it was there. Such a thing would have been unthinkable in a United Methodist parsonage in the South twenty-five years ago.

Last Saturday night my wife, Marianne, and I went to a Sunday school class potluck dinner party. The invitation said that each couple or single was to bring a dish. Nothing was said about beverages. Fifteen couples attended. All fifteen brought at least one bottle of wine. The hostess had prepared three pitchers of iced tea, just in case. The tea went virtually untouched over the course of the evening.

We have come a long way on the alcohol issue during the last quarter century. By *we,* I mean Protestants of the more conservative denominational traditions. Catholics, Greek Orthodox, Episcopalians, and Lutherans have never been overly concerned with teetotalism. At my nephew's wedding at a Catholic church in Atlanta in the early nineties, even I was a bit shocked to see an open bar in the fellowship hall at the wedding reception. As an old joke that ministers like to tell puts it: Methodists will drink, but not in church. Baptists will drink, but not in public. Catholics will drink anywhere.

As more and more health benefits have come to be associated with the moderate drinking of wine, the traditional antialcohol stance of many Protestant churches needs to be rethought. Preaching total abstinence should now be considered irresponsible. Moderate consumption of alcohol should be the accepted norm, in church and out of church, just as it was when Qoheleth wrote and in Jesus' time. My octogenarian mother-in-law is losing her sight because of macular degeneration. The church preached against alcohol when she was growing up, so she never drank alcohol until recent years. Recent medical research, though preliminary, indicates that people who drink red wine regularly and in moderation almost never get macular degeneration. If the Methodist Church had not preached against it and my mother-in-law had been a moderate drinker of red wine, she most probably would not be going blind now.

Wine in the Song of Solomon

The most beautiful love poem ever written is the Songs of Songs, better known to most people as the Song of Solomon. The language and imagery of the poem are utterly gorgeous. Read aloud and listen to the alliteration of the Hebrew in its opening line: *shir ha shirim asher leshelomo* (the song of songs which is Solomon's). The sensuality of the words throughout the poem echoes the sensuality of their meanings. This poem about the love of a man and a woman is charged with sexual imagery.

Both Judaism and Christianity have had a lot of trouble with the Song of Songs. Its overt sexuality and utter lack of any apparent religiousness have bothered those with ascetic tendencies in both religions. The way out has been to read the poem as an allegory of the love of God for Israel or of the love of Christ for the Church. The poem itself never mentions God or Israel or Christ or the Church. In the middle ages, the preaching of the allegorical interpretation of the Song of Songs became extremely popular. One of the church's strictest ascetics, St. Bernard of Clairvaux, preached hundreds of sermons on the Song of Songs without ever recognizing in it the sexual love of a man and a woman. Commentators on the Song of Songs in the last half of the twentieth century finally came to the conclusion that the poem really is about human love and sexuality.

Although there is much we could say about human sexual love in this poem, our focus here will be on what the poem says, both literally and metaphorically, about wine. The book contains only the lyrics of the poem, but there are implied parts for different readers: a man, a woman, and a chorus. In some places it is not entirely clear which speaker has which part. It begins with the words of the woman, "Let him kiss me with the kisses of his mouth!" (Song 1:2). The next lines are spoken by the chorus, apparently an all-female chorus, to the woman:

> For your love is better than wine,
> your anointing oils are fragrant,
> your name is perfume poured out;
> therefore the maidens love you (Song 1:2–3).

The woman then says to the chorus, "Draw me after you, let us make haste. The king has brought me into his chambers." The chorus then responds, "We will exult and rejoice in you; we will extol your love more than wine; rightly do they love you" (Song 1:4).

In these opening verses, the chorus twice compares the woman's love to wine. They say to the woman that her love is better than wine and that they will extol her love more than wine. As fine and wonderful a thing as wine is, the woman's love is even finer. The implication of the comparison is that wine and the woman's love share some common characteristics. Anyone who has experienced the pleasures of good wine and of genuine love would readily grasp the similarity. Drinking good wine and making love with someone whom you deeply love are among life's finest pleasures. Both have an intoxicating effect. Both lift us out of the ordinary experiences of day-to-day living into a more richly pleasurable experience that makes up for all the drudgeries of daily life. Yet as pleasurable, delightful, and joyous as the experience of drinking good wine is, the experience of deeply felt sexual love is greater.

The wine and sexual love comparison is continued in chapter 5 by all three speakers. The man begins:

> I come to my garden, my sister, my bride;
>   I gather my myrrh with my spice,
> I eat my honeycomb with my honey,
> I drink my wine with my milk.

The chorus then chimes in:

> Eat, friends, drink,
>   and be drunk with love.

And then the woman speaks:

> I slept, but my heart was awake.
> Listen! My beloved is knocking.
> "Open to me, my sister, my love,
>   my dove, my perfect one;
> for my head is wet with dew,
>   my locks with the drops of the night."
> I had put off my garment;
>   how could I put it on again?
> I had bathed my feet;
>   how could I soil them?
> My beloved thrusts his hand into the opening,
>   and my inmost being yearned for him.
> I arose to open to my beloved;
>   and my hands dripped with myrrh,
> my fingers with liquid myrrh,
>   upon the handles of the bolt.
> I opened to my beloved (Song 5:1–6).

The references to myrrh require explanation. Myrrh is a fine perfume—another of life's pleasures. In fact, myrrh was the finest perfume of antiquity. It is derived from a gum resin that comes from several species of shrubs and trees of the genus *Commiphora*. Myrrh can be tapped directly from its sources and does not require any refining or blending with other elements. Though used primarily for perfumes, myrrh had numerous other uses. Like frankincense, it could be burned as incense (see Exod. 30:34 and Song 3:6), and in a time long before the seventeenth-century invention of soap, when clothes could be washed only with water, myrrh was sometimes used to make clothes smell better (see Ps. 45:8). It was also used as a beauty treatment for women (see Esther 2:12), and could be mixed with wine to drink as a painkiller; such a mixture was given to Jesus while he hung on the cross (see Mark 15:23). It was also used with other perfumes and spices for embalming (John 19:39). Its fine fragrance, which led some to believe that it had healing properties, resulted in its being called "the balm of Gilead." Whatever its usage, myrrh was always considered to be one of the finer things in life and was always costly. In the nativity story in the Gospel of Matthew, it is one of the gifts that the wise men brought to the baby Jesus.

As a perfume, myrrh had an aphrodisiac quality. It could be ground into powdered form or sipped as a liquid. In the powdered form, it was often put into a cloth sachet and worn between a woman's breasts, and indeed the woman in the Song of Songs compares her beloved to "a bag of myrrh that lies between my breasts" (Song 1:13). Both the myrrh and the beloved have aphrodisiac qualities. It is worth noting that the Song of Songs is far and away the most olfactory book of the Bible. Myrrh is one of many fragrances and fragrant plants and flowers mentioned in the Song of Songs. All of these were deeply pleasurable to the people of biblical times, more pleasurable than we moderns can know. We have soap. This wonderful and highly underrated invention enables us regularly to cleanse our bodies and clothes. In antiquity people were far more accustomed to smelling bad than we are. That made people who smelled good highly desirable indeed.

Throughout the passage, the thinly veiled sexual imagery conveys the sheer excitement of both the man and the woman as they thrill to their encounter. For our purposes, I want to note especially the association of wine with honey, milk, myrrh, and spice as being among the most pleasurable things in life, pleasures that compare with that even greater pleasure of human sexual love. The chorus affirms this sentiment to the two lovers when they say, "Eat, friends, drink; / and be drunk with love." Lovemaking is as pleasurably intoxicating as drinking good wine, even more so. The chorus encourages the two lovers to drink deeply, both of the good wine and of their love for each other.

Within the beauty of the Song of Song's love lyrics, wine plays an accompanying role. Just as a crisp chardonnay with distinct notes of pear is the perfect accompaniment to a summer lunch of fish and fruit, so a fine wine is the perfect accompaniment to romantic love, either in lyrics or in life.

Wine and the Prophets

Scholars have long recognized that the Book of Isaiah is really three books by at least three different authors. The first Isaiah, from whom the book takes its name, is Isaiah of Jerusalem, a prophet who lived in the eighth century B.C.E. and prophesied from 738 to 701. The thrust of his prophecy was the forthcoming doom and destruction of Jerusalem and all the land of Israel at the hands of foreign oppressors. The total fulfillment of his prophecy came in 586 B.C.E., when the Babylonians, under their powerful king Nebuchadnezzar, destroyed the city of Jerusalem and led its survivors away into captivity in Babylon. In his prophetic portrait of the forthcoming devastation, Isaiah says:

> Therefore a curse devours the earth,
>   and its inhabitants suffer for their guilt;
> therefore the inhabitants of the earth dwindled,
>   and few people are left.
> The wine dries up,
> the vine languishes,
>   all the merry-hearted sigh.
> The mirth of the timbrels is stilled,
>   the noise of the jubilant has ceased,
>   the mirth of the lyre is stilled.
> No longer do they drink wine with singing;
> strong drink is bitter to those who drink it.
> The city of chaos is broken down,
> every house is shut up so that no one can enter.
> There is an outcry in the streets for lack of wine;
> all joy has reached its eventide;
> the gladness of the earth is banished (Isaiah 24:6–11).

Although this is only one of many oracles with which the prophet Isaiah dooms the people of Jerusalem, it frighteningly portrays one sad aspect of the coming war's devastation. Wine and music, like most of the finer things in life, are products of leisure. Though they bring joy, they are not essential for life.

When there is no leisure—and in time of invasion, there is no leisure—there is no time to produce and enjoy wine and music.

Food, water, and sleep are the necessities of life. Unrelenting toil in menial work is the lot of far too many people. In times of war or natural disaster, life tends to be reduced to these most basic necessities. When all human energy is expended on gaining the necessities for day-to-day existence, nothing of enduring quality can be created as a legacy for subsequent generations. In contrast, when all the needs of a society can be produced by a relatively small number of its members, more and more time is left for the creation and production of those nonessentials that immeasurably enrich people's lives. Those nonessentials include, among hundreds of other things, music, art, architecture, literature, skilled craftwork, philosophy, and even wine.

Life throughout most of antiquity was lived at the level described in the quotation from Isaiah: sustenance living with no time for leisure. Warfare wreaked continual havoc on most ancient societies. At a few times and places in antiquity, things did not follow the normal course of tedium. The Golden Age of Greece, which more properly should be called the Golden Age of Athens, was the finest example. In this period the people of Athens created the highest civilization the world had ever known, pushing civilization ahead in virtually every field.

In art, for example, the classical Greek style emerged. With its emphasis on the perfection of form, dynamic sculptures such as Myron's "Discus Thrower" replaced the rigid, lifeless forms of earlier Greek, Egyptian, and Near Eastern sculpture.

In architecture, the Golden Age produced the most beautiful building of all antiquity, the Parthenon. Resting majestically atop the Athenian acropolis, this massively heavy stone edifice appears light. From every side and every distance, its supporting columns appear perfectly straight, perfectly the same size, and perfectly equidistant from one another. Amazingly this effect is achieved through optical illusion. In reality, the columns differ in size, straightness, and distance from one another in incredibly precise ways. If they were perfectly straight, perfectly the same size, and perfectly equidistant, they would not look it. These two brilliant architects had a far greater understanding of optics than has anyone before them and scarcely anyone since. The effect is stunning.

In philosophy it was the age of Socrates and Plato. The twentieth-century British philosopher Alfred North Whitehead once described the entire Western philosophical tradition as "a series of footnotes to Plato." Plato's extensive works, which are extant in their entirety, provide the basis, define the categories, and set the standards for Western philosophy to this day.

In literature the Golden Age saw the writing of the Greek tragedies and comedies: the works of Aeschylus, Sophocles, and Aristophanes, and the early works of Euripides. Plays like *Oedipus Rex, Antigone,* and *Medea* set the dramatic form that endures to the present day in the West, and probed the deepest themes in human experience.

The achievements of the Golden Age could not have occurred without a large measure of leisure. Socrates was a day worker on the construction of the Parthenon. But at leisurely dinner gatherings with the men who formed his circle of friends, he pondered the deepest of philosophical questions, as well as questions that to some—but not to Socrates—seemed trivial. Socrates and his compatriots debated, for example, whether "cookery" is an art. That the question was even raised demonstrates, in a small way, the movement from society to civilization. As cooking moves from the necessary labor of preparing essential nourishment to the superb art and skill of creating feasts of magnificent flavor and beautiful presentation, so also society moves to civilization.

The society in which Jesus lived was not nearly so advanced. Under the yoke of Roman colonial rule and the constant fear of fruitless rebellion, the Palestinian Jews, among whom Jesus lived, mostly eked out a subsistence living from the land. Jesus would give them a taste of the good life. He would do his part to move them from society to civilization.

The message of Jesus was foreshadowed in the Book of Isaiah, particularly in the writings of the "Second Isaiah," who wrote chapters 40–55 a century and a half after Isaiah of Jerusalem prophesied. The situation of the Jewish people had utterly changed from the time of Isaiah of Jerusalem to that of the Second Isaiah. The destruction foretold by the first Isaiah had come to pass. After a decade of Babylonian domination, the Jews of Jerusalem revolted. King Nebuchadnezzar dispatched the Babylonian army to put down the revolt with a vengeance. They destroyed Jerusalem. Solomon's Temple, which had stood for four hundred years as the center of all Jewish worship, was razed to the ground. Those whom the Babylonians did not kill, they took away into slavery in exile. They caught the last Jewish king, Zedekiah, fleeing with his family to Egypt. They then killed each of his ten sons, one by one, before his eyes. Their deaths were the last things he would see, for they then cut his eyes out and took him away in chains to Babylon.

The Babylonian Exile lasted from 586 to 538 B.C.E. In the course of those years, the Jews living in slavery lost their native language and came to speak the Babylonian tongue, Aramaic. They also lost much of their culture. But at least some of them held fast to faith in their God and to the memory of Jerusalem, to Zion (the hill on which Jerusalem stood), and to what their life had once been. They would pass both that faith and that memory on to their children. Psalm 137, a psalm of the exile, beautifully expresses the tenacity of their memory:

> By the rivers of Babylon—
> there we sat down and there we wept
> when we remembered Zion.
> On the willows there
> we hung up our harps.
> For there our captors
> asked us for songs,
> and our tormentors asked for mirth, saying,
> "Sing us one of the songs of Zion!"
> How could we sing the Lord's song
> in a foreign land?
> If I forget you, O Jerusalem,
> let my right hand wither!
> Let my tongue cling to the roof of my mouth,
> if I do not remember you,
> if I do not set Jerusalem
> above my highest joy (Psalm 137:1–6).

The exile ended when the mighty Persian Empire conquered the Babylonians. Their great king Cyrus set the Jews free and allowed any who wished to return to Jerusalem. Cyrus was such a hero to the Jews that the Second Isaiah even called him by the Hebrew word *messiah,* God's anointed (Isa. 45:1).

The Second Isaiah wrote toward the end of the Babylonian Exile, about 540 B.C.E. He clearly perceived that the exile was about to end and looked forward to the postexilic return to Jerusalem and an abundantly better life for the Jewish people. As pessimistic as were the doom prophecies of the First Isaiah, the Second Isaiah's prophecies are filled with vibrant hope and optimism. He wrote in jubilant tones about the coming freedom of the people and the restoration of Israel.

In his last chapter, which many scholars view as an invitation to abundant life, he mentions wine. He writes using the standard prophetic messenger speech, that is, in the first person—I—with that first person being God. The prophet is simply conveying God's message:

Ho, everyone who thirsts,
    come to the waters;
and you that have no money,
    come, buy and eat!
Come, buy wine and milk
    without money and without price.
Why do you spend your money for that which is not bread,
and your labor for that which does not satisfy?
Listen carefully to me, and eat what is good,
and delight yourselves in rich food.
Incline your ear, and come to me;
    listen, so that you may live.
I will make with you an everlasting covenant,
my steadfast, sure love for David (Isaiah 55:1–3).

The Second Isaiah envisions a time of wealth and prosperity for all. Not only will bread—that is, the basic foods for the sustenance of life—be free, but luxury foods such as wine will be free. Not only will these people, who have been near starvation in their slavery, have all they need to eat, they will have even more. They will be able to delight themselves in rich food. God will make a new and everlasting covenant with them.

The Second Isaiah foreshadows much that will be in the ministry of Jesus. In the Gospel of John, Jesus will say, "I came that they may have life, and have it abundantly" (10:10). Far from wanting to bring a pleasure-denying asceticism to his followers, Jesus wants to bring an abundance of the good things of life. We see this particularly in his story of turning water into wine at the wedding feast at Cana, in Galilee.

WINE IN THE LIFE OF JESUS

The drinking of wine was a significant part of the daily life of Jesus and most other people who inhabited the Mediterranean world of antiquity. Wine was a basic agricultural commodity, traded as widely as olive oil or grain. Because no form of refrigeration, not even ice in the winter, was available in the mild Mediterranean climate, fruits, vegetables, meats, and milk were produced and consumed locally. Wine, oil, and grain could be traded over greater distances.

The wines of antiquity were almost entirely red. The ancients had developed a fairly good knowledge of viticulture. They knew how to trellis, and they knew how to prune the vines so as to force more of the root nutrients into the grapes and less into the leaves. Unlike our romantic images of purple-footed grape crushers, the ancients used wine presses. They understood fermentation and cool storage, and they knew that good wine improved with age. They made large and often beautifully decorated amphoras for storing wines. They knew to fill the amphoras to the top and seal them to keep oxygen out. The most basic difference between ancient wine making and wine making today is that the ancients did not age their wine in wooden barrels.

The Galilee region that was Jesus' home had significant wine production. Wine was more plentiful in Galilee than in the rocky, arid region of Judea to the south, where the holy city of Jerusalem stood. Judea bought its wine from Galilee.

The Wedding Feast at Cana

According to the Gospel of John, the first miracle that Jesus performed was turning water into wine at the wedding feast of Cana. None of the other Gospels records this miracle. Though it is quite possible that none of the others knew the story, it seems equally as likely that they omitted the story intentionally, because it did not fit the portrayal of Jesus that they wanted to put forth. It is the only miracle of Jesus' that could be described strictly as a pleasure miracle. Most of his miracles involved healing the sick. His miraculous feeding of the five thousand with bread and fish was to provide necessary sustenance to the crowd. The wedding feast at Cana provided a miracle of more complex motivation.

Throughout history, weddings have been a cause for celebration, and wine has long been associated with celebration. Besides its wonderful flavors, wine contains alcohol, a substance that tends to have a relaxing effect on both the brain and the body and that tends to make people happy. First-century Jewish wedding feasts were similar to our own (except that we now call them inappropriately "receptions," rather than feasts). An abundance of wine and food was provided for the guests.

New Testament scholars disagree as to the historicity of this miracle story. To those who deny the possibility that Jesus or anyone else could transcend the laws of nature to perform miracles, this story cannot be historical. Even to those who grant the possibility of Jesus being an authentic miracle worker, this particular miracle story might not be considered historical. Further, it is singly attested; that is, it appears in only one Gospel source. Multiple attestation, such as we find with the story of the feeding of the five thousand, gives greater grounds for historicity. This miracle does not cohere well to the rest of the miracle traditions in the Gospels. It does not heal anyone. It does not combat the powers of evil. It is utterly unnecessary. Moreover, this miracle has possible symbolic connotations, which may have occasioned its literary creation and composition.

Despite these scholarly reservations, I would affirm the essential historicity of the miracle. At the very least, the miracle surely reflects the authentic sensibilities of the historical Jesus. He graced this wedding feast with his presence and blessed its abundance of wine. Indeed he may very well have turned the water into wine.

John's Gospel tells the story:

> On the third day there was a wedding in Cana of Galilee, and the mother of Jesus was there. Jesus and his disciples had also been invited to the wedding. When the wine gave out, the mother of Jesus said to him, "They have no wine." And Jesus said to her, "Woman, what concern is that to you and to me? My hour has not yet come." His mother said to the servants, "Do whatever he tells you." Now standing there were six stone water jars for the Jewish rites of purification, each holding twenty or thirty gallons. Jesus said to them, "Fill the jars with water." And they filled them up to the brim. He said to them, "Now draw some out, and take it to the chief steward." So they took it. When the steward tasted the water that had become wine, and did not know where it came from (though the servants who had drawn the water knew), the steward called the bridegroom and said to him, "Everyone serves the good wine first, and then the inferior wine after the guests have become drunk. But you have kept the good wine until now." Jesus did this, the first of his signs, in Cana of Galilee, and revealed his glory; and his disciples believed in him (2:1–11).

This miracle has a number of striking and unusual things about it. First, in contrast to most of the rest of the Gospel of John, in which Jesus seems to know everything he is going to do and everything that will happen as a result, here Jesus seems to be acting on the spur of the moment. Second, Jesus' response to his mother seems a bit gruff and impersonal, as well as somewhat cryptic. What does he mean by, "My hour has not yet come?" Third, although John calls this miracle the first of Jesus' signs in Galilee that revealed his glory, it can reveal his glory only to the readers of the story, not to most of the people who were present at the wedding feast. Jesus performs the miracle anonymously. Only the servants who had drawn the water, Jesus' mother, and the disciples who were there, knew that Jesus had worked a miracle. The chief steward clearly did not know where the wine had come from. The wedding guests, including the bride and groom, were apparently oblivious to the whole event. They never even knew that the wine had run out. Fourth, John obviously intends some significance in noting that the six stone jars were holding the water for the Jewish rites of purification. What is that significance?

Jesus' mother (she is never called by her name, Mary, anywhere in the Gospel of John) becomes aware that the wine has run out and conveys this information to Jesus. She seems to know that he has the power to do something about this lack of wine. In the brief conversation that ensues, she and Jesus seem to be talking on different levels. She is simply concerned about the wine having run out; he is concerned about the time for the full revelation of his glory.

Such dual-level conversations are a common motif in the Gospel of John. When Jesus talks to Nicodemus in John, chapter 3, about being "born again" or "born from above," Nicodemus thinks Jesus is talking about going back into the mother's womb and literally being born again. In John, chapter 4, when Jesus is talking to the Samaritan woman at the well, she thinks his offer of living water that will make her never thirst again is literally water, which she thinks will relieve her of the burden of drawing water daily from the well. In these and several other cases in the Gospel of John, Jesus speaks on a spiritual level, while the people he is conversing with are stuck in literalism.

Jesus appears a bit perturbed when his mother pushes him to create more wine for the feast. He seems to have his own idea about the timing of the progressive revelation of his divine glory, and her wish to have him perform a miracle now does not fit. Nonetheless, he acquiesces to his mother and quietly, anonymously, unceremoniously, and without magical incantation or evoking the name of God or laying on of hands, he miraculously transforms the water into wine. Scarcely anyone at the feast knows what has happened.

Then the chief steward, whom we might consider to be the manager of the catering service, tastes the water that has become wine. He calls the bridegroom, thinking that it is the bridegroom who has reserved this exceptionally good wine for this late point in the feast. He then says to the bridegroom, "Everyone serves the good wine first, and the inferior wine after the guests have become drunk. But you have kept the good wine until now." The statement has a symbolic meaning, in addition to its obvious literal meaning. On the symbolic level, Jesus is the bridegroom who has brought the good wine to the feast. (Later in the New Testament, in Eph. 5:21–32, the relationship between husband and wife is compared to the relationship between Christ and the Church.) The water becoming wine symbolizes the abundance of God's grace, which overflows to all God's people with the coming of Jesus.

The story ends without another word from Jesus or his mother. We never hear a word from either the bride or the groom. John simply closes the story with this summary statement, "Jesus did this, the first of his signs, in Cana of Galilee, and revealed his glory; and his disciples believed in him." Jesus' glory is revealed through this story to all who read it, but at the wedding feast itself, his glory was revealed secretly and quietly to only a few servants who saw and understood what had happened. The rest of the people there benefited in pleasure from what Jesus had done, even though they did not know that he had done it.

Another point of interest to our discussion is the sheer amount of wine that Jesus makes. Each of the six water jars contains twenty to thirty gallons. Jesus thus makes 120 to 180 gallons of wine, *after* the guests have already consumed a considerable amount of wine. That would be equivalent to six hundred to nine hundred bottles of wine today. This is a huge amount of wine. Even if it were a large wedding feast—which is not likely because Cana was a very small town—this amount of wine was far more than the wedding guests would ever have been able to drink. Though this may symbolize the great abundance of God's grace, it also shows that Jesus quite literally wanted to bring to these wedding guests an abundance of human pleasure. As Jesus says in John 10:10, "I came that they might have life, and have it abundantly."

A final and most crucial point in this story, which all too many readers seem to miss, is that the water Jesus turns into wine is no ordinary water. It is water that is poured into special jars for the Jewish rites of purification. The Jewish Torah contains a vast amount of legal material—613 laws in all. Many of these laws concern matters of ritual impurity and rites of purification. Many different things can make a person ritually impure. Touching unclean animals or eating foods that come from them is one example. Foods deemed unclean include pork, shrimp, oysters, and any other kind of crustacean or shellfish. A woman is ritually impure or unclean during menstruation and during pregnancy. A man is unclean after a seminal emission. Anyone who touches an unclean person becomes unclean. Some people were permanently unclean: anyone with a chronic skin disease, such as the lepers with whom Jesus frequently associated, was considered to be permanently unclean. Although ritual impurity is not the same thing as sin, it is something that requires remedy. That remedy is ritual washing in waters of purification. A ritual washing cleanses a person of impurity and allows that person to stand before God in a place of holy worship.

Jesus frequently challenged the laws of ritual purity followed by his fellow Jews. Jesus said that it is not what goes into a person's mouth that defiles a person, but what comes out of a person's mouth. It is not what you eat that makes you impure, it is what you say and think. In Mark's Gospel, the author comments, "Thus [Jesus] declared all foods clean" (7:19).

Many righteous Jews, especially the priests, would have been very upset with Jesus if they had known he used waters reserved for purification to make a vast amount of wine for a wedding feast. Jesus was far more interested in pleasure than in purity laws.

Many Christians throughout the ages have, in my view, missed the point of Jesus' action at the wedding in Cana. Jesus was a man of pleasure. He wanted to bring the physical pleasures of this world to everyone, but especially to the poor and the sick, who rarely experienced them. A tepid church-basement punch-and-cookies wedding reception was not for him. Weddings are among the times of greatest human celebration. People save up money and spend lavishly on weddings, not just in our society but also in a vast number of countries, cultures, and religions throughout the world. Jesus knew that wine was one of the chief elements of a good celebration. He wanted the celebration at this wedding in Cana to have more than enough wine, and good wine at that. So he made it happen. He made it happen without fanfare. He did not show off before the wedding guests. Neither did he use this wedding as an opportunity to preach. He did not draw people's attention to the miracle and tell them to give all the glory and credit for it to God. He simply enabled the people to have a great time. That is what a celebration is for.

A Glutton and a Drunkard

Jesus was not the only unorthodox Jewish religious leader of his time. During their own lifetimes, John the Baptist may have been more widely known than Jesus. Both leaders were unorthodox, but they were very different from each other. John's message and practice were simple, direct, and straightforward. Jesus was far more subtle and complex. John preached and practiced a baptism for the repentance of sins in the wake of God's impending fiery judgment. He demanded that all who heard him repent and be baptized lest they be tortured and burned with the fires of Hades in the life to come. John lived an ascetic life. He was very likely a Nazirite, a member of an ancient order of Jewish men whose vows included celibacy and prohibited wine and strong drink. The Gospels tell us that John came out of the wilderness of Judea, clothed in a roughly woven garment of camel's hair. He lived on a nonagricultural diet of locusts and wild honey. The few fragments we have of his fiery sermons contain a consistent message: "Even now the ax is lying at the root of the trees; every tree therefore that does not bear good fruit is cut down and thrown into the fire" (Luke 3:9). "I baptize you with water; but one who is more powerful than I is coming; I am not worthy to untie the thong of his sandals. He will baptize you with the Holy Spirit and fire. His winnowing fork is in his hand; to clear his threshing floor and to gather the wheat into his granary; but the chaff he will burn with unquenchable fire" (Luke 3:16–17). Judgment, John preached, will be fast and fierce at the hands of a soon-to-arrive messianic figure.

John's message was utterly devoid of love—God's or anyone else's. John's mission was without miracle. He saw little point in teaching people how to live better, more abundant lives, for the judgment was near, and life was too short to worry about. He had no concern for this life, only for the next. He certainly had no concern for the pleasures of this life. He likely held the Puritan's view that pleasure is the prelude to sin. The Gospels record but one meeting between John and Jesus. It is not entirely clear whether he knew that Jesus was the messiah he awaited. John was arrested and decapitated at the very beginning of Jesus' ministry. Had he lived longer, he would have seen Jesus' ministry emerge as something radically different from his own.

Although John may not have known of these differences, the people of Galilee certainly noticed them. Jesus himself commented on the differences: "For John the Baptist has come eating no bread and drinking no wine, and you say, 'He has a demon'; the Son of Man has come eating and drinking, and you say, 'Look, a glutton and a drunkard'" (Luke 7:33–34). These statements imply that Jesus had been compared unfavorably to John the Baptist. The Jewish public admired John the Baptist for his asceticism, and disparaged Jesus for his love of pleasure. Jesus never denies the charges, exaggerated as they may be. Although he never disparages John the Baptist, and indeed honors him, Jesus does not at all mind the public's making a distinct separation between John and him.

Later Christian tradition, and even much of modern New Testament scholarship, would want to see the closest possible relationship between Jesus and John. Many modern scholars see John as Jesus' mentor. The Jewish people of Jesus' time knew better. Unlike John, Jesus did not expect an imminent end of the world and final judgment. Unlike John, Jesus believed in the essential goodness of the world, of people, and of life. The whole purpose of his teaching was to show people the way to the good life in the here and now. Denial of the God-given pleasures of this life was not a part of Jesus' plan for humanity. Jesus did not say, "I came that you may deny life, and deny it abundantly." Jesus taught the joy of the simple pleasures of this life, pleasures he believed should be available to all people, not just the rich and powerful, not just the healthy, and not just those who were considered pure by Jewish law.

Even people who recognize the validity of Jesus' most important statement, "I came that you may have life, and have it abundantly" (John 10:10), often misconstrue it as referring to eternal or spiritual life rather than physical life. Jesus did not make such a separation between spiritual life and physical life. For him they were all bound up into a single thing. Unlike John the Baptist, who healed no one, Jesus spent most of his ministry healing people of their physical and mental diseases. These healings were not just raw demonstrations of divine power; they were loving and caring actions that enabled people to live better lives. Jesus knew that people could not fully enjoy the pleasures of this life if they were living in pain and torment. His ministry sought to take away the obstacles that keep us from attaining the good life.

New Wine in Fresh Wineskins

Jesus contrasted his teaching with that of the ascetic John the Baptist on another occasion:

> Now John's disciples and the Pharisees were fasting; and people came and said to him, "Why do John's disciples and the disciples of the Pharisees fast, but your disciples do not fast?" Jesus said to them, "The wedding guests cannot fast while the bridegroom is with them, can they? As long as they have the bridegroom with them, they cannot fast. The days will come when the bridegroom is taken away from them, and then they will fast on that day.
>
> "No one sews a piece of unshrunk cloth on an old cloak; otherwise, the patch pulls away from it, the new from the old, and a worse tear is made. And no one puts new wine into old wineskins; otherwise, the wine will burst the skins, and the wine is lost, and so are the skins; but one puts new wine into fresh wineskins" (Mark 2:18–22).

Jesus' language here is highly symbolic, and the symbols imply a complex of meanings rather than a single interpretation. The one historical point these verses make clear is that Jesus and his disciples were not ascetics. They did not fast. In fact, throughout the Gospels Jesus never commands fasting, never has a single good thing to say about fasting, and has several negative things to say about it. Jesus and his disciples enjoyed the pleasures of the good life and did not practice any sort of ritual self-denial.

Jesus' metaphors of the patch and the new wine have surface meanings that are fairly obvious. As for their deeper meaning, two common interpretations of these parables are, first, that the new message of Jesus cannot be contained in the old wineskin of Judaism, that the structures of Judaism must be replaced; and second, that the new message of Jesus will not fit in this old sinful world in this old sinful age, but that this world must be apocalyptically destroyed and replaced by a new one that would be filled with the message of Jesus. I doubt that Jesus intended either of these meanings.

The patch and the new wine are indeed the message of Jesus, the message of the goodness of life for all who would follow him. The old garment and the old wineskin symbolize old ways of living. These old ways of living include asceticism, exclusivism—be it racial, national, ethnic, gender, class, or religious—and hatred. We cannot accept the teachings of Jesus without accepting a significant change in our life. That change is not merely a spiritual belief about Jesus and God; it is a positive change to the way we live in the present. We will talk more about that change in the chapter on the greatest pleasure, love.

A crucial point that is rarely mentioned in a discussion of the image of new wine is that Jesus uses wine as a symbol of his teaching. Jesus could have used water, a substance essential for the sustenance of life, instead. He could have talked about putting fresh water into a cracked water jar. Much of the symbolism would have been the same. Jesus chose to use wine, not water, as a metaphor for his teachings. This choice of metaphor says a lot about how Jesus understood his teachings and how Jesus understood wine. Water is essential for life; wine is not. Water sustains our bodies; wine gives us pleasure. The message of Jesus is not essential for our lives. We can live, we can even live good lives, without it. But if we fill our lives to the full with Jesus' message, we can live in a new, intoxicated state of deeper joy and fullest pleasure.

The Last Supper

In the parable of the wine and the wineskins, Jesus used wine as a symbol for his teachings. At his last supper with his disciples, he used wine as a symbol for himself. The earliest telling of the story of the Last Supper comes from the pen of the Apostle Paul, who, in his first letter to the Church at Corinth, wrote:

> For I received from the Lord what I also handed on to you, that the Lord Jesus on the night when he was betrayed took a loaf of bread, and when he had given thanks, he broke it and said, "This is my body that is for you. Do this in remembrance of me." In the same way he

> took the cup also, after supper, saying, "This cup is the new covenant in my blood. Do this, as often as you drink it, in remembrance of me" (1 Cor. 11:23–25).

Once again Jesus could have chosen water for the symbol of the new covenant in his blood. Water, as well as wine, would likely have been drunk at meals. His choice of wine was made easier by two considerations. First, if the Last Supper is a Passover meal, as the Gospels of Matthew, Mark, and Luke suggest, then cups of wine were employed in the ritual. Second, wine is the color of blood; water is not.

I would contend that there was more to it than these practical considerations. Jesus wanted his disciples to drink wine as a reminder of him after he was gone. The deep, rich, complex flavors of a good red wine would remind Jesus' followers of the pleasures they experienced in his presence. Drinking this wine would remind them of their new covenant with him, that is, their agreement to follow his teachings of love. Finally, drinking the wine would remind them of Jesus, the man himself. "Like a fine wine that goes down smoothly over lips and tongue," so the experience of Jesus was and is totally good and pleasurable. It is neither exaggeration nor sacrilege to say that the true Christian celebration of the Last Supper is like a toast to Jesus.

Conclusion

Our tour through biblical attitudes about wine, in both the Old and New Testaments, leads to two clear conclusions. First, the people of both testaments immensely enjoyed the fruit of the vine. They took great pleasure in wine making and wine drinking, and considered wine to be one of the finer things life had to offer. Wine was a gift of God's goodness and a part of all that God wants humanity to enjoy. Second, drunkenness, the abuse of wine, is not what God desires. We must be clear in our understanding that abuse and addiction are far removed from Jesus' acceptance of wine as one of the pleasures of life. As with any pleasure, it should be accepted as a gift and enjoyed wisely and moderately.

There is much that we do not know about alcoholism. We know how alcoholism operates in individual people. We know about its individual, family, and social consequences, but we have much to learn about its origins. Do some individuals and ethnic groups have a genetic predisposition to alcoholism, or is it a product of cultural expectations and practices? Most of the French and the Italians, for example, drink significant quantities of wine every day, and the French in particular begin drinking wine with meals at a very young age. Yet the incidence of alcoholism is much lower among the French and Italians than among Americans. Although we cannot answer such questions yet, it is plain to see that a world of difference exists between drinking for the sole purpose of getting drunk and slowly sipping a fine wine for its magnificent flavors and the way it so beautifully accompanies good food. Yet fine wine is one of life's great pleasures, and it was understood as such by the people of the Old Testament and by Jesus himself.

4 / JESUS AND WOMEN

Jesus immensely enjoyed the pleasure of the company of women. In this respect, as in so many others, he was radically out of step with the mores of his time. Jesus lived in a Middle Eastern culture that understood women to be the property of their husbands or fathers and to be distinctively inferior to men. Girls married shortly after reaching the age of puberty. Their province was the home; they ventured from it only to procure the daily supplies for household living or to visit with relatives. They had few social relationships apart from familial ones. They did not converse with men other than male relatives. They dressed modestly, with all the body covered except for the face and hands. They seldom traveled beyond their own village or town. The role of and limitations on women in many Middle Eastern societies today has scarcely changed from what it was in Jesus' time.

In that time, unmarried women and widows with no father or adult son to care for them had to find the means of earning a living. The most common means were prostitution, begging, or indenturing oneself to a family as a domestic servant or slave. A few skillful women were able to establish their own small businesses.

Women had few basic rights. Although they could buy and sell property on behalf of their husbands, rarely could they own it; few Jews in Palestine owned property anyway. A woman could own property only if she inherited it from her husband when there was no other male relative in the family. Women had few legal rights. A husband could easily divorce his wife, send her away penniless, and keep the children. The wife had no legal recourse. Furthermore, she was from that point on treated as an object of shame in the community. Women could not hold any sort of office or position of leadership. In a society that was 85 to 90 percent illiterate, women had a much higher illiteracy rate, perhaps 95 percent.

To be sure, there were exceptions. Women who came from royalty or from families of great wealth had opportunities that were not available to other women. For example, the brilliant Cleopatra, Queen of Egypt, who died twenty-seven years before Jesus was born, was fluent in fourteen languages. She was one of the last people who could read the ancient Egyptian hieroglyphics, a writing system that had fallen into disuse eight centuries earlier. Cleopatra effectively administered a considerable though waning empire. For years she managed to hold off the vast juggernaut of the rapidly expanding Roman Empire, until her forces finally fell to the Romans at the Battle of Actium in 31 B.C.E. Though other women may have existed during the time of Jesus who were as brilliant as Cleopatra, they never had the opportunity to show it.

For the vast majority of women in the ancient Mediterranean world, life was hard and tedious, full of physical drudgery. They had no plumbing or electricity, agriculture was at subsistence level, and there was scarcely any treatment for disease. Houses, streets, and people were always filthy. Because they had no birth control, women could spend their entire adult lives pregnant or nursing babies. Few women lived beyond the age of menopause, and it was not at all uncommon for a woman to have had twenty or more pregnancies. From those twenty pregnancies, only about four to six children were likely to survive to adulthood.

The Jewish religion and culture, of which Jesus was a part, based its mores on a code of purity. We saw earlier that the ritual purity laws in the sacred books of the Torah had a clear impact on the lives of women. A woman was ritually impure much of the time. She was impure during menstruation and during the entire time of pregnancy. While she was impure, men were not to touch her, and had little or no contact with her.

For anyone, male or female, who stood outside the cultural norms for one reason or another, life was even harder. To be handicapped or to have a chronic skin disease made one impure for a lifetime. Such people were usually separated from the rest of society and forced to live in even worse conditions.

The purity codes were not the only thing that separated people in Jesus' time. Society was also divided into strict social classes. Jesus lived in a Palestine that was under the oppressive authority of Roman rule. The occupying Roman military forces considered themselves superior to all Jews, whom they regarded as dirty, barbaric, and uncivilized. They felt particular contempt for the Jewish religion, with its insistence on limiting the number of gods to one and its refusal to accept any representational art, which the Jews considered to be forbidden graven images.

Jewish society itself provided further class delineations. The priests were the highest social class. They owned most of the available land. They exacted tithes (a religious word for taxes) from the peasants who worked the land. Though the priests and a few nonpriestly men of wealth and family prestige represented less than 2 percent of the Palestinian Jewish people, they owned more than 90 percent of the land and wealth. Other classes included a small middle class of merchants and a lower middle class of skilled artisans. The vast majority of the Palestinian Jews, perhaps 90 percent, were landless peasants with few possessions who lived in hovels. They had no means of improving their lot in life; they worked incredibly long hours merely to subsist. They could not move up in the social scale. By law they could not become priests because the priesthood was hereditary. The few who possessed extraordinary talents or skills could conceivably work their way into the artisan or merchant class, but that rarely happened; class structures were too rigid. It was these landless peasants whom Jesus referred to as "the poor," and whom he constantly blessed. It was to these poor that Jesus sought to bring the pleasures.

Jesus was born and grew up in this harsh, strict society. From what we can gather in the Gospels, he appears to have been born into the artisan class. As we noted earlier, he was a *tekton,* traditionally translated in English Bibles as "carpenter," although "builder" is probably the more accurate translation. Very likely Joseph and Jesus and his brothers were trained as stonemasons.

Jesus was one of very few people who moved from one social class to another. He voluntarily moved down. He left the artisan class for the peasant class. He chose to spend the entire time of his ministry among the peasants and with those who were even lower than the peasants, the handicapped and the diseased.

Although Jesus had some occasions for interactions with people of higher classes, and even with Romans, he treated all people as equals. To Jesus the lowest leper was as good as King Herod Antipas, the ruler of Galilee. A woman was as good as a man. Jesus questioned and rejected the class structures and purity codes of his time. We do not know at what point in his life he began this questioning; the Gospels tell us nothing about his teen years and his twenties. He emerges in the Gospel narratives at age thirty with his thought on these matters already fully formed and radically different from the thinking of anyone else of his time.

Though much could be said about Jesus' relationships with the poor, the diseased, the handicapped, and the mentally ill, the focus of this chapter is on his relationships with women. The Gospels, insofar as we know, were all written by males. Even though these male writers shared the dominant male values of the culture, their Gospels, especially Luke's, are amazingly full of stories about Jesus and women.

THE WOMEN APOSTLES

All the canonical Gospels portray Jesus as having selected a group of twelve men as his disciples. They and other men who knew Jesus during his lifetime would later come to be known as the apostles. The title by which Jesus is most frequently called in the Gospels is *rabbi,* a Hebrew word meaning "teacher." There were many other rabbis in Jesus' time. They were not priests; unlike the priests, they did not have to come from a particular tribe of Israel, and they did not become rabbis by heredity. A Jewish man became a rabbi by becoming a disciple of a rabbi. During his period of discipleship, he would learn from the more experienced rabbi the laws of the Torah, the oracles of the prophets, the traditions of the Jewish people, and the sayings of the rabbinic fathers. After his period of discipleship, if he had shown himself to be an extraordinarily good rabbi, he would gather a group of disciples of his own and begin to teach them.

Although we know nothing of Jesus' life between the ages of twelve and thirty, it seems altogether likely that he spent part of that time learning the scriptures and traditions of the people as a disciple to an older rabbi. It is even conceivable that he could have been a disciple of the greatest rabbi of that time, Hillel, who died about 20 C.E., when Jesus was twenty-four years old. Some of the sayings and ideas of Jesus' show remarkable similarity to the sayings of Hillel. For example, Hillel said, "Do not do unto others as you would not have them do unto you." Jesus' statement, which Christians call the Golden Rule, simply eliminates the use of the word *not* in Hillel's saying.

Some similarities, and numerous differences, existed between Jesus and the other rabbis of the time. One significant difference is that Jesus was an itinerant rabbi. Other rabbis were located in a particular place, where their students would come to live and study with them. More were in Jerusalem than anywhere else. But one dramatic difference between Jesus and the other rabbis is particularly notable: Jesus taught women.

Although Jesus did not engage in a head-on confrontation with the rabbis and the culture on this point, the Gospels are replete with examples of his teaching women and treating them as equals to his male disciples. This included having women disciples who, like his male disciples, followed him in his itinerant ministry. Unlike the male disciples, these women disciples paid for their tutelage under Jesus and gave money for his and the other disciples' financial support. The Gospel writers do not publicize these facts, which were something of an embarrassment for both the early Christians and the other Jews they were trying to convert. Luke, however, does tell us the basic facts:

> Soon afterwards he went on through cities and villages, proclaiming and bringing the good news of the kingdom of God. The twelve were with him, as well as some women who had been cured of evil spirits and infirmities: Mary, called Magdalene, from whom seven demons had gone out, and Joanna, the wife of Herod's steward Chuza, and Susanna, and many others, who provided for them out of their resources (8:1–3).

Luke does not tell us exactly how many are the "many others," but it would be fair to guess that Jesus had about as many female as male disciples. The Gospels have little to say about most of the male disciples. Some, such as James son of Alphaeus, Bartholomew, Thaddeus, and Simon the Cananaean, are simply mentioned once by name; no stories are told about any of them. Three of the male disciples—Peter, James, and John—form an inner group that is closer to Jesus and are the leaders of the disciples. It is likely that a corresponding triumvirate of leadership existed among the women disciples, with the three whom Luke mentions by name being the leaders: Mary Magdalene, Joanna, and Susanna. Of the three leading male disciples, Peter was foremost. It was of Peter that Jesus said, in Matthew 16:18, "You are Peter [*Petros* in Greek], and on this rock [*petra* in Greek] I will build my church." Mary Magdalene appears to have held the corresponding position of leadership among the women disciples. She followed Jesus throughout his Galilean ministry. She followed him to Jerusalem for the last week of his life, she stayed at the cross until his death, and she was at his tomb on the Sunday morning of the resurrection. Like Peter's, her name is usually mentioned first in any listing of women disciples (see, for example, Mark 16:1, Luke 24:10).

In the books of the New Testament other than the Gospels, the disciples come to be called apostles. This designation goes beyond the twelve to include other followers of Jesus, almost all of whom knew Jesus during his lifetime on earth. Christians throughout the centuries have customarily assumed that those who were named apostles were all men. Indeed this has been the principal argument of Pope John Paul II against the ordination of women priests in the Roman Catholic Church. In fact, this is not the case. One woman is specifically called an apostle by Paul in the final greetings of his letter to the Romans. He writes in Romans 16:7, "Greet Andronicus and Junia, my relatives who were in prison with me; they are prominent among the apostles, and they were in Christ before I was." Although Andronicus and Junia are otherwise unknown to us, they appear to be an apostolic married couple, like the frequently mentioned Priscilla (also called Prisca) and Aquila (see Acts 18:18,26; Rom. 16:3; 1 Cor. 16:19). Paul's greeting makes it clear that it is not just Andronicus but his wife, Junia, as well who are not only considered apostles but prominent among them.

This passage was so embarrassing to the Oxford and Cambridge dons who created the English translation of the Bible called the King James Version, that they changed the woman's name *Junia* to the pseudo-male name *Junias*. Of course, there was no such person as Junias, and in all of ancient Greek and Roman literature, we do not find a single example of a man with the name Junias. The translators simply made the name up.

Because Paul says that Junia was "in Christ" before he was, and because he calls her an apostle, it seems altogether probable that she was one of the "many other" women that Luke claims were disciples of Jesus'. We shall return to the leaders of this group, Mary Magdalene, Joanna, and Susanna, after a look at the lives of some other women who were important to Jesus.

MARY AND MARTHA OF BETHANY

In addition to the itinerant men and women disciples, Jesus had women and men disciples who remained living in a particular location. A prime example is the siblings Mary and Martha of Bethany and their brother, Lazarus. Bethany is a village located a short distance from Jerusalem, just on the other side of the Mount of Olives. The three siblings lived together in a house there. None of them appears to have been married. Luke provides us with a brief but telling narrative about the lives of the two sisters and their relationship with Jesus:

> Now as they went on their way, he entered a certain village, where a woman named Martha welcomed him into her home. She had a sister named Mary, who sat at the Lord's feet and listened to what he was saying. But Martha was distracted by her many tasks; so she came to him and asked, "Lord, do you not care that my sister has left me to do all the work by myself? Tell her then to help me." But the Lord answered her, "Martha, Martha, you are worried and distracted by many things; there is need of only one thing. Mary has chosen the better part, which will not be taken away from her" (10:38–42).

In this passage Jesus makes a bold feminist statement. Though the two sisters were indeed real historical characters, and the story bears all the markings of authenticity, the sisters are also representative figures for two very different understandings of womanhood. Martha bears all the traditional traits of a first-century Jewish woman. She understands her place and sees her role within Jewish society as keeper of the house. She wants to show all appropriate, gracious Middle Eastern hospitality to the important guest she is entertaining. Jesus' visit to her home appears not to have been planned beforehand. She has not had time to prepare the home, as she would have liked to for this special guest. She is counting on her sister, Mary, to help her quickly get things in order. She becomes upset when Mary does not help. There may be a background of disagreement between the sisters on the relative importance of good housekeeping, but Luke does not tell us anything to this effect.

While Martha plays the role of the traditional Jewish woman, Mary is anything but. When Luke says that she "sat at the Lord's feet and listened to what he was saying," he casts her in a totally different role from that of her sister. Luke's early readers, particularly his Jewish readers, would immediately understand this sentence in a way that would not be readily apparent to modern readers. Sitting at the feet of a master and listening to his words was exactly what a rabbi-in-training would do as a disciple to a master rabbi. In contrast to Martha, the traditional Jewish housekeeper, Mary plays the utterly untraditional role of rabbi and disciple of Jesus.

Modern readers usually take Martha's rebuke of her sister as an implication of laziness and irresponsibility on Mary's part. Ancient Jewish readers would have heard it as a rebuke of Mary's pretending to be a rabbi and disciple of Jesus and a rejection of her role as a traditional Jewish woman. When Martha asks Jesus to tell her sister to reassume the proper role for a traditional woman, she is no doubt astonished by Jesus' response. His response is not the expected rebuke of Mary, nor is it a rebuke of Martha. Rather, it is a disavowal of the traditional role of women in Jewish society as the only option for women: "Mary has chosen the better part, which will not be taken away from her."

When I gave this interpretation of the Mary and Martha story to a college class on Jesus a few years ago, a young conservative Christian woman, who did not believe that women should be in the Christian ministry, became highly distraught. She told me that I was missing the point of the story. The point of the story, she said, is that Mary saw that it was more important to focus one's attention on Jesus than on the secular affairs of daily life, such as housekeeping. Martha's being "distracted by her many tasks" meant that we should not be distracted by all our day-to-day work, but should focus our attention more acutely on Jesus and his teachings, just as Mary did. My student's interpretation of the story is not entirely off the mark. Certainly Luke thinks that one should focus one's attention more on the teachings of Jesus than on housekeeping. But her interpretation misses the radical thrust of the story's meaning. It thus sadly misunderstands Jesus' view of women and the message that Jesus' understanding of women has for us today.

Jesus' last sentence makes the story's message clear, "Mary has chosen the better part." Like a part in a play, we could say that Mary has chosen the better role. It is a better role for a woman to be a rabbi than a housekeeper. This is not to say that being a housekeeper is not a good and acceptable role for any woman (or man) who wants that role. But the better role is for women to become educated, to learn from masterful teachers, and to train for careers in society, including the career of ministry.

Mary and Martha each play roles in two other stories about Jesus. First is the story of the raising of their brother, Lazarus, in John, chapter 11. The second, which I will focus on here, is the story of the anointing at Bethany, in John, chapter 12. The story occurs at the beginning of the last week of Jesus' life. At the home of Mary, Martha, and Lazarus, a dinner was given in honor of Jesus. Guests at the dinner included at least some of the disciples. Martha, taking her customary role, served the dinner. While the guests were at the table, "Mary took a pound of costly perfume made of pure nard, anointed Jesus' feet, and wiped them with her hair. The house was filled with the fragrance of the perfume" (John 12:3).

Mary's action, which seems strange to twenty-first-century people, was far less strange in its first-century context. In a time centuries before the invention of soap, the natural odors of human bodies were far more prominent in daily life than they are today. In antiquity people customarily washed their feet before entering houses, but an honored guest was likely to receive special treatment. This appears to have been the case with Mary and Jesus. She had bought him a gift of expensive perfume. Just as a woman today might receive an expensive necklace when being honored at a dinner, so Mary put the expensive perfume on Jesus' feet to honor him at this dinner.

With perfume dripping from Jesus' feet, and perhaps lacking a cloth to wipe them, Mary wiped his feet with her hair in a gesture of deep love and care for him. Between his feet and her hair, the whole room became filled with the pleasant scent of the fine perfume, a scent that would enhance the pleasure of the entire evening.

Mary's act of love immediately provoked a negative reaction from one of the male disciples, Judas Iscariot, who said, "Why was this perfume not sold for three hundred denarii and the money given to the poor?" (12:5). In Mark's version of the story, which has some significant differences from John's, Jesus at this point says:

> "Let her alone; why do you trouble her? She has performed a good service for me. For you always have the poor with you, and you can show kindness to them whenever you wish; but you will not always have me. . . . Truly I tell you, wherever the good news is proclaimed in the whole world, what she has done will be told in remembrance of her" (Mark 14:6–9).

John tells us that Judas was entirely dishonest in his statement, and that he really wanted the money for himself and not the poor, because he was the keeper of the group's treasury. Be that as it may, Judas's words display a common ascetic dislike of things pleasurable and expensive. Mary certainly could have found some much less expensive perfume, which, even if it did not fill the room with luxurious fragrance, would still have the necessary deodorizing effect. But Jesus was a man of pleasure, a man who thoroughly enjoyed the pleasures of this world and sought to bring the pleasures of this world within the reach of all people. He knew that life was short, and that his own life in particular was likely to be very short. He knew that the pleasures of this life are for this life—the next life will have its own pleasures. Moreover, he knew that Mary's gift was given in love, and love is not to be rejected.

THE WOMAN AT THE WELL IN SAMARIA

In addition to stories of the women disciples, the Gospels also tell of a number of encounters between Jesus and various other women. In the fourth chapter of the Gospel of John we read of an encounter between Jesus and an unnamed woman whom he meets at a well in Samaria. The ensuing narrative shows Jesus in vigorous opposition to two of the major prejudices of his time.

Jesus' own people, the Jews, like virtually every other group in antiquity, were ethnocentric. They considered themselves to be the chosen people of God. They considered all other peoples to be unclean. They made little distinction among the other peoples. One word covered them all, *goyim,* which we translate "gentiles." One distinction they did make among the gentiles was with Samaritans. The rest were bad, but Samaritans were worse.

The Samaritans were descended partly from the ancient people of Israel. After the death of King Solomon, in 922 B.C.E., a civil war broke out in Israel, with the ten Hebrew tribes of the North fighting to secede from the two tribes of the South, where the capital city of Jerusalem was located. This civil war ended with a permanent split. The Northern Kingdom, called Israel, would never again be united with the Southern Kingdom, called Judah. This separate existence of the two Hebrew kingdoms lasted two hundred years. It came to an end in 722 B.C.E., when the Northern Kingdom was destroyed by the overwhelming military power of the empire of Assyria. The Assyrians scattered most of the inhabitants of Israel in exile across the face of their vast empire, and brought other conquered peoples to dwell in what had been Israel, along with the relatively few Hebrews who were left there. These scattered Israelites would become known as the ten lost tribes of Israel. They would never exist again as a group or a nation. The mixture of conquered peoples sent into exile into what had been the Northern Kingdom eventually intermarried with the Hebrews who were left, and formed what came to be called the Samaritans. The Samaritans adopted the Hebrew religion.

The Hebrews of the Southern Kingdom were spared the horrors of the Assyrian conquest. Before the Assyrians could take Jerusalem, the encroaching armies of a vast new empire, Babylonia, threatened them to the east. The Assyrian King Sennacherib had to withdraw all his troops from the siege of Jerusalem in 701 to fight what would be a long and bloody war with Babylonia, a war the Assyrians lost in 612 B.C.E. After conquering Assyria, Babylonia captured the Southern Kingdom in 597. Ten years later they destroyed the city of Jerusalem, including Solomon's temple, which had stood as the center of Jewish worship for four centuries. They sent the Jews of the Southern Kingdom into exile in Babylonia. Unlike the Hebrews of the former

Northern Kingdom, the Jews of the South maintained their ethnic national identity and their religion, even in exile. When Babylon was conquered by Persia, a new and even mightier empire, in 538 B.C.E., Persia's King Cyrus allowed the exiled Jews to return to their homeland.

The Jews who returned found Jerusalem to be an uninhabited pile of rubble overgrown with scrub vegetation. They built a second temple on the spot where Solomon's temple had stood, but it was a shabby structure, a far cry from the glory Solomon's temple had been. The returned exiles encountered the Samaritans to the north. Many intermarried with Samaritan people, but others regarded Samaritans as a mongrel people, a mixture of racial and ethnic groups who were more unclean than other gentiles. This latter view prevailed. The powerful priest Ezra eventually commanded all Jewish men who had married Samaritans to divorce their wives and send them and their children away to Samaria. Ezra saw the ethnic purity of the Jewish people as the will of God. The eminently impure Samaritans would thus become more despised than anyone else by the Jews.

The proximity of these two ethnic groups who shared the same basic religion further fostered their mutual enmity. The Jews lived in Galilee, the northernmost region of Palestine, the place where Jesus grew up and began his ministry. The Jews also lived in Judea, to the south, the land of the holy city of Jerusalem. The Samaritans lived in the middle. Jewish antipathy toward the Samaritans was so strong that Jews would usually travel between Judea and Galilee by going across to the other side of the Jordan River and traveling a longer road, which enabled them to avoid Samaria altogether.

When Jesus encounters the woman at the well in Samaria, he shows blatant disregard for the two prevailing prejudices of his people in his day: Jewish men do not talk to women other than female family members, and Jews avoid Samaritans altogether. In this story Jesus has an extended conversation with a Samaritan woman:

> A Samaritan woman came to draw water, and Jesus said to her, "Give me a drink." (His disciples had gone to the city to buy food.) The Samaritan woman said to him, "How is it that you, a Jew, ask a drink of me, a woman of Samaria?" (Jews do not share things in common with Samaritans.) Jesus answered her, "If you knew the gift of God, and who it is that is saying to you, 'Give me a drink,' you would have asked him, and he would have given you living water." The woman said to him, "Sir, you have no bucket, and the well is deep. Where do you get that living water? Are you greater than our ancestor Jacob,

who gave us the well, and with his sons and his flocks drank from it?" Jesus said to her, "Everyone who drinks of this water will be thirsty again, but those who drink of the water that I will give them will never be thirsty. The water that I will give will become in them a spring of water gushing up to eternal life." The woman said to him, "Sir, give me this water, so that I may never be thirsty or have to keep coming here to draw water."

Jesus said to her, "Go, call your husband, and come back." The woman answered him, "I have no husband." Jesus said to her, "You are right in saying, 'I have no husband'; for you have had five husbands, and the one you have now is not your husband. What you have said is true!" The woman said to him, "Sir, I see that you are a prophet. Our ancestors worshiped on this mountain, but you say that the place where people must worship is in Jerusalem." Jesus said to her, "Woman, believe me, the hour is coming when you will worship the Father neither on this mountain nor in Jerusalem. You worship what you do not know; we worship what we know, for salvation is from the Jews. But the hour is coming, and is now here, when the true worshipers will worship the Father in spirit and truth, for the Father seeks such as these to worship him. God is spirit, and those who worship him must worship in spirit and truth." The woman said to him, "I know that Messiah is coming" (who is called Christ). "When he comes, he will proclaim all things to us." Jesus said to her, "I am he, the one who is speaking to you" (John 4:7–26).

This conversation is immensely intriguing in numerous respects. The first thing to note is that it is the longest conversation Jesus has with anyone in any of the Gospels. His longest recorded conversation is with a foreign, impure woman whom he had never met before.

Second, the woman consistently misunderstands Jesus throughout the conversation. What is even more striking is that Jesus makes little effort to correct her misunderstandings. The misunderstandings do not result from cultural differences; rather, in every case they result from the woman's wanting to take Jesus literally, when he is speaking not literally but spiritually.

Her first misunderstanding appears in her question, "How is it that you, a Jew, ask a drink of me, a woman of Samaria?" She is thoroughly acculturated to the prejudicial customs of her time and place, and assumes that Jesus is as well. Why is he flaunting those long-held customs? She thinks of him only as another Jewish man, men who have snubbed her own people always and oppressed them whey they had the opportunity. She does not understand yet that she is dealing with no ordinary Jewish man, but a man who goes far beyond the bounds of Judaism, even beyond the bounds of humanity. She does seem to learn fairly quickly that this man has none of the customary prejudices.

Her second misunderstanding revolves around the use of a particular Greek word, *zo-on*, which the NRSV translates consistently as "living" (we get our words *zoo* and *zoology* from it). The word also has common idiomatic use when paired with the word for water. What we call *running* water, they called *zo-on hydor,* or "living water." What we call *still* water, they would think of as "dead water." The Greek idiom *living water* may sound a bit odd to us, but surely it is no more odd than our own English idiom, *running water.* Water does not run; it has no legs or feet. It flows. Both we and the Greeks would be more accurate, if less colorful, to say "flowing water." When Jesus says to the woman at the well, "You would have asked him, and he would have given you living water," she understood him to mean running water, as opposed to the still water in the well. She continues to misunderstand when Jesus says, "Everyone who drinks of this water will be thirsty again, but those who drink of the water that I will give them will never be thirsty. The water that I will give will become in them a spring of water gushing up to eternal life." Her response, "Sir, give me this water, so that I may never be thirsty or have to keep coming here to draw water," clearly displays her lack of comprehension.

Few of us today know the drudgery of hauling water from a well to a house. Water is remarkably heavy. People, even ancient people, use a lot of it. In antiquity, as in many third-world countries today, hauling water takes up a significant portion of a woman's time and energy. The Samaritan woman thought that Jesus was offering her some magic *eau de vie* that would eliminate both her thirst and her need to haul water.

Jesus was talking about something else. However vaguely we may comprehend his meaning in the use of the words *living water,* we know that he did not mean H_2O. What did he mean? Jesus does not tell the woman what he means, and the author of the Gospel of John does not tell us what Jesus means. As with much that Jesus says, he leaves it to us to figure out what it means.

Here is a common understanding. Ancients, as well as moderns, knew that no life could exist without water. Water is the essence of life. It makes up 80 percent of the molecules in our body. Jesus uses the essential nature of water as a metaphor for what he was truly offering the Samaritan woman: a life-giving spirit, one that is as available to us now as it was to her then.

The story leaves us hanging. Jesus gives no further explanation of living water to the woman. Does she ever come to grasp his meaning? We cannot know. On the other hand, does she even need to grasp his meaning? If what he does for her by his very presence one day in her life brings her the life-giving spirit, then the fountain of living water will continue to spring forth within her, regardless of whether she understands the theological meaning of it all.

Jesus then changes the conversation. He shows the woman that he perceives her whole life, including the embarrassing fact that she has had five husbands and is currently living with a man who is not her husband. Jesus states this simply as a matter of fact. He in no way condemns her for circumstances that in both the Jewish and the Samaritan religious understandings would have constituted an immoral life.

They then talk about a key difference between Jews and Samaritans, namely the central worship shrine for each religion. For the Jews it was the temple in Jerusalem; for the Samaritans, Mt. Gerizim. This would not be an issue of significance for any of us today, but for the Jews and the Samaritans, it was crucial. Sacrifices to God could be made only at the central worship shrines, and sacrifice—that is, animal sacrifice—was the central act of worship. The Jews regarded Samaritan sacrifices as illegitimate and utterly unpleasing and unappeasing to God because they were made at a place that was not holy. The Samaritans, though they did not similarly discredit the Jerusalem temple, did claim the legitimacy of their own sacrifices.

Jesus sees both the Jews and the Samaritans as wrong on this issue. True worship depends neither on the place where nor the manner in which it is done. Jesus says that the true worshippers will worship "in spirit and truth." He further makes the shockingly bold statement that "God is spirit." He is not saying that God has a spirit, or that there is a Spirit of God or Holy Spirit. He is not saying that people perceive God through the spirit.

Both the Jews and the Christians thought of God in human terms, often in grossly human terms. For example, in Genesis 3:8, Adam and Eve, "heard the sound of the LORD God walking in the garden at the time of the evening breeze." One gets the impression of some sort of mythological half-human, half-divine bigfoot. Like the Egyptian, Canaanite, and Greco-Roman gods, the God of the early Jews and Christians displayed the all-too-human emotions of jealousy and rage as often as divine love. The ancients had difficulty conceiving of God in any manner beyond the human. The idea of God as spirit lay beyond the borders of their imaginations. A few ancient people, such as the brilliant Greek philosopher Plato, could get beyond the humanoid representations of God. But in a society that was never much more than 15 percent literate and had no printing press, few people in antiquity were ever able to read Plato's ideas. A first-century Jewish genius from Alexandria named Philo did.

Jesus never did. Jesus, however, was able to come to the understanding that God is spirit without direct help from Greek philosophy. He found it as difficult to communicate this understanding to the everyday people he dealt with as Plato did. Understanding God in the abstract is difficult for us. It is so much easier to think of God as a quasi-human. Jesus called on the Samaritan woman to get beyond her humanoid theology. Did she? This story in the Gospel of John does not tell us but leads us to think—not quite. The woman struggles to grasp the meaning of his words, "God is spirit, and those who worship him must worship in spirit and truth." This kind of thinking is totally new to her. She is already struggling from the shock of having this strange Jewish man talk to her. More difficult still is the struggle to understand the meaning of his words. Though she does not think that she can understand his meaning, she thinks that she might in the future, "I know that Messiah is coming," she says, "When he comes, he will proclaim all things to us." In her thinking, long conditioned and deeply ingrained by her Samaritan religious beliefs, the coming messiah will make everything crystal clear. Jesus answers her, "I am he, the one who is speaking to you."

A vast array of thoughts must have poured through her mind at that moment. This mysterious man, a Jew no less, claimed to be the messiah of the Samaritans. Was he serious? Was he right? Was he crazy? Was she crazy? Perhaps he was "proclaiming all things to her," but he was not *explaining* all things to her. He was pushing her to the limits of her theological imagination, pushing her beyond literalism, pushing her where she had little confidence to go. She would have to rethink God and everything about God. Could she do it? Jesus thought she could. Jesus thinks more highly of our intellectual and theological abilities than we are willing to ourselves.

These few moments of the woman's deepest thought in her entire life were interrupted by the return of the disciples, whose astonished expressions unmasked their deep consternation at finding Jesus speaking with a woman. Not wishing to listen to what she knew was about to occur—an all-male argument with her as the focus of disagreement—she left her water jar and returned to the city. To the all too dull day-to-day life of her town, she is happy to provide a little gossipy excitement. To everyone she sees, she exclaims, "Come and see a man who told me everything I have ever done! He cannot be the Messiah, can he?" (John 4:29).

This is the last we hear of the Samaritan woman. Does she reform her style of living? Does she revise her style of thinking? John does not tell us. Most likely he does not know. Jesus thought she would. I think she did. Although she was almost surely illiterate and uneducated, Jesus thought she was capable of a deeper understanding of God. He surely thinks that all of us are capable of much deeper theological thinking than most of us are ready to pursue.

The story of Jesus and the woman at the well in Samaria shows us so much about so many things. This little discourse about it does not begin to do it justice. It is about much more than Jesus and his relationships with women, but for our purposes it is in this area that we shall draw some conclusions. In sum, the story tells us these things about Jesus and women: Jesus, unlike virtually everyone else of his time, treated women equally with men. Jesus does not limit his love for women to women of his own religious and ethnic group. He does not limit his love for women to women whose moral behavior matches what society deems acceptable. Jesus had women friends from the upper echelons of Jewish society, such as Joanna, the wife of King Herod Antipas's steward Chuza, but his encounter at the well in Samaria demonstrates that he loved the company of women from all strata of society. Perhaps most important, Jesus considered all women as well as all men—from every societal and educational background—to be able to think theologically, to be able to become philosophical theologians, to be able to understand that "God is spirit."

LIFE AND DEATH, A WOMAN AND A GIRL

The story originates in Mark 5:21–43. Matthew and Luke both adapted it from Mark (see Matt. 9:18–26 and Luke 8:40–56). Mark has actually combined two healing stories. Historically they may have happened at different times, but for thematic reasons, Mark has put them together. The combined stories illustrate Jesus' care for women, and in particular his concern for women's health.

Jairus, one of the leaders of the Capernaum synagogue, and a man of no little importance in local Jewish society, found himself in a desperate situation. His twelve-year-old daughter was sick to a point near death. Apparently nothing could be done to save her. Dealing with an itinerant faith healer was doubtless not his primary course of action. But desperate situations demand desperate measures. Whether one should believe in faith healers is not the question one asks when all else has failed. Jairus was willing to try anything. He went to Jesus and begged him, the text says, "repeatedly" to come and heal his daughter. Although we are not told why Jesus did not go immediately with Jairus, it seems likely that Jesus was too busy healing others in the crowd that

Jairus had made his way through. Jairus was surely feeling that time was running out for his daughter. Jesus knew differently. Finally Jesus went with Jairus, and a large crowd followed them.

While they were on their way to Jairus's house, a woman with a serious gynecological problem, a menstrual flow that had never stopped in twelve years, despite her having seen numerous physicians and spent all her money seeking a cure, approached Jesus from behind. Not feeling herself worthy to request help directly from the healer, or perhaps embarrassed to ask because of the nature of her problem, the woman reached out and touched his garment, somehow sensing that merely touching Jesus might bring her relief. As soon as she touched him, her bleeding stopped. Mark says that Jesus was immediately aware that power had gone forth from him. Curiously, Jesus does not seem to be aware of who it was that had touched him. He turned around in the crowd and asked, "Who touched my clothes?" (Mark 5:30). The disciples ask him how he can expect to find who touched him when such a crowd is surrounding him. At that moment the woman came forward and told her story. Jesus then said to her words that surely surprised the disciples and should surprise us, "Daughter, your faith has made you well; go in peace, and be healed of your disease" (5:34). We shall return to these words of Jesus' in a few moments.

At this point some people who have come from Jairus's house tell Jairus, Jesus, and the crowd that there is no need for Jesus to go any farther, that Jairus's daughter is dead. Jesus then said to Jairus, "Do not fear, only believe" (Mark 5:36). He dismissed the crowd, allowing only the inner circle of his disciples, Peter, James, and John, to go with him into Jairus's house. The people in the house were weeping and wailing over the death of the little girl. Jesus said to them that she was not dead but only sleeping. He then asked them to leave. Going with Jairus and three disciples into the room where her lifeless body lay, Jesus said, "Little girl, get up!" (Mark 5:41). At his words she arose and walked. Mark then tells us that the girl was about twelve years old.

These combined healing stories are interesting in a number of respects. Most New Testament scholars think that the stories originally circulated independently, and that Mark put the two together in a typical Markan literary device, which some scholars anachronistically call a "Markan sandwich." Mark has sandwiched the story of the healing of the woman with the menstrual problem between two halves of the story of the healing of the little girl. He has not done so haphazardly, but with the clear literary intent of wanting his readers to see the connections between the two stories.

There are several connections. There are also several disconnections. The first and most obvious connection is that both of the healed are female. Most ancient healers did not bother with healing women. Females were not considered significant enough for them to expend their powers on. As we have seen, Jesus treated females equally with males.

Second, neither of the females in the story is named. Only the name of the little girl's father is mentioned. Does this not contradict the first point, that Jesus treated both sexes equally? No, for Jesus is not telling the story; Mark is. Mark is merely displaying his culture's predisposition for regarding only the names of important people as worthy of note. Throughout his Gospel many males who are healed are also left unnamed. He names only people of social importance and people, male and female, who have an ongoing relationship with Jesus.

A third similarity, not significant for modern Christian readers but very important for the ancient Jewish culture of which Jesus was a part, is that both these females were ritually unclean at the time that Jesus came in contact with them. By Jewish law a woman is unclean during the entire time of menstruation. A corpse is unclean. When the unclean woman touched Jesus, she made him unclean. It is clear in Jewish law that being unclean is not the same thing as being sinful. One does not need to repent for ritual uncleanness. One does, however, have to separate himself or herself from others during times of ritual uncleanness. People who are ritually clean are to refrain from contact, insofar as is possible, with people who are unclean. When the time of a person's uncleanness is completed, the person undergoes a purification rite to become ritually clean again. All this is spelled out in the Books of Leviticus and Deuteronomy in the Old Testament.

When, in Mark 5:27, the menstruating woman touched Jesus, she made him unclean. When, in Mark 5:41, Jesus took the hand of the dead little girl, he became unclean. In neither case does Mark record Jesus undergoing a ritual washing to purify himself from his uncleanness. In fact, none of the Gospels record Jesus undergoing a Jewish ritual washing for purification. Although he once told a leper whom he had healed to go to the priest for ritual cleansing (Mark 1:44), he did so to demonstrate to the priest that the former leper was no longer a leper and could undergo ritual cleansing, not because he believed in following the ritual cleanness laws. Indeed Mark will later say, in 7:19, that Jesus "declared all foods clean," no longer supporting the Jewish prohibition of pork, shellfish, and other foods that the Torah declares to be unclean.

A fourth similarity is the curious detail of the number twelve. The woman's menstrual flow has continued unabated for twelve years. The little girl is twelve years old. Are these two "twelves" merely coincidental? Perhaps they are. Perhaps they are nothing more than the catchwords that led Mark to put the two stories together. I would be more inclined to say that they were coincidental if the number were eleven or thirteen, but twelve is the most symbolically significant number for the earliest Christians. There were twelve tribes of Israel, and Jesus chose twelve disciples. The New Testament Book of Revelation, written about the same time as the Gospel of Mark, is filled with symbolic numbers. Twelve is, for example, symbolically the number of the people of God. In Revelation, John includes a vision of a woman with a crown of twelve stars on her head. This woman gives birth to the messiah. Could Mark be making a subtle statement that women, even women considered unclean by Jewish law, are in every respect as much the people of God as are men?

There are also some differences between the two healings. The healing of the woman could be called unintentional on the part of Jesus. His final comment to her, "Your faith has made you well," rather than "My divine power has healed you," indicates the surprising idea that the woman was instrumental in her own healing. This was not the case with the little girl, who played no part in her own healing. Although the healing of the woman appears to have come about through the touch of Jesus' garment (and by extension the touch of Jesus himself), the healing of the little girl came about through the words of Jesus. It is noteworthy that throughout the Gospels there is no single manner by which Jesus heals people. He does not use magical incantations or formulas like some other healers of his time. Sometimes he lays his hands on people to be healed; sometimes he merely speaks to them; sometimes he even heals people at a distance.

In the middle of the twentieth century, some biblical scholars sought scientifically plausible scenarios for biblical miracles. This can be achieved more easily with some miracles than others. When, for example, Elisha, in 2 Kings 4:34, encounters the apparently dead son of a Shunammite woman, he "lay upon the child, putting his mouth upon his mouth, his eyes upon his eyes, and his hands upon his hands; and while he lay bent over him, the flesh of the child became warm." What to the ancients was miracle appears to us as mouth-to-mouth resuscitation. Perhaps Jesus did not really turn water into wine at the wedding feast at Cana, but the intoxication of the evening made it seem like the wine never ended. Perhaps the cessation of the woman's flow of blood came through biofeedback that her newly found faith in Jesus enabled her to employ. Perhaps Jairus's daughter was not really dead but only comatose, and Jesus hit the right pressure point in her wrist as he took her hand so that her heart, lungs, and brain resumed normal functioning.

Other miracles are not so readily rationalized. Lazarus had been dead for four days, and his tomb had begun to smell of the decomposition of his body when Jesus raised him to life (John, chapter 11). In recent years, scholars have largely lost interest in positing such pseudoscientific explanations of biblical miracles. Some simply deny the authenticity of biblical miracles, while others choose to hold the question open and leave the miracles unexplained.

It is not the purpose of this study to deal with the scientific and historical questions of the authenticity of any of Jesus' healings. Like most historians, I regard the question of whether miraculous healings are possible to fall outside the realm of questions that historians can definitively answer. What is important for this study is not so much what happened scientifically in these stories but what they tell us about Jesus.

Jesus' compassion went far beyond the normal cultural limitations of class, gender, religion, and ethnicity that characterized his day. Women were important to him, all women, young and old. Women's health issues were important to him. Ritual purity laws of the Torah were not important to him. Jesus had never met either of the women he heals in Mark, chapter 5. They were of no special importance to him or to society. They were ordinary human beings like you and me. Jesus was willing to employ extraordinary means to heal these ordinary people.

The medical profession today, when it is at its best, is like Jesus in this way. Doctors, nurses, and hospitals go to extraordinary measures to preserve the lives of tiny prematurely born infants whose parents may be of any social stratum, including the poor. The medical procedures may cost hundreds of thousands of dollars, which the parents will never be able to pay, but everything possible to save the infant's life is done anyway. And of course it makes no difference whether the infant is a boy or a girl.

In some cultures today, in segments of society where females are devalued, medicine is not practiced equally for males and females. News stories tell us of frequent infanticide of girls in India, so-called female circumcision in Africa, and all sorts of repressive measures used against women in fundamentalist Muslim countries, especially Afghanistan in the years it was ruled by the Taliban.

It seems never to have occurred to Jesus that he should treat women as unequal to men, even though his culture was filled with such inequalities. Within a generation of his death, his followers would begin to revert to the sexual discrimination that was prevalent in the culture and call it Christian. Within a century Christianity would turn misogynistic, and much of Christianity remains misogynistic to this very day. Fortunately not all branches of Christianity have closed themselves to the feminist movement. One or two have even gone so far as to be as feminist as Jesus.

JESUS AND THE WOMAN WHO WAS A SINNER

In Luke 7:36–50 we read the strange story of Jesus' deeply personal encounter with an unnamed woman described as a sinner. The story bears some remarkable similarities to the story of the anointing at Bethany as told in the Gospel of John (but not as it is told in Matthew and Mark). But this story does not occur in Bethany, and the woman who anoints Jesus' feet in this story is not Mary of Bethany. Some later Christian tradition would identify the woman in Luke's story as Mary Magdalene, even though the story itself makes no such identification. Mary Magdalene is an important character in Luke's Gospel. If she had been the woman in this story, Luke surely would have identified her.

At one of the villages in Galilee, Jesus was having dinner with a Pharisee named Simon. Although the Pharisees were his most frequent opponents in Galilee, Jesus never showed any prejudice against them as a group, and was more than willing to socialize with them. The next part of the story is striking:

> And a woman in the city, who was a sinner, having learned that he was eating in the Pharisee's house, brought an alabaster jar of ointment. She stood behind him at his feet, weeping, and began to bathe his feet with her tears and to dry them with her hair. Then she continued kissing his feet and anointing them with the ointment (Luke 7:37–38).

This is a story with so many improbable factors that it seems more than possible that it actually happened. A good Pharisee would never have let such a woman into his house, especially when he had a guest, and especially at the time of a meal. Pharisees are especially strict about not eating with people who are ritually impure. Contrary to popular belief, nothing in this story says that the woman was a prostitute, only that she was a sinner. By the word *sinner,* early Jewish readers of this text would know that Luke was talking about a woman who had not undergone the Jewish ritual washings for purification of her sins. She would thus be totally unacceptable in the house of a Pharisee. Another possible understanding of *sinner* in this passage is that she was a gentile. All gentiles were permanently ritually impure, and thus were considered sinners. Even if she were not a sinner, she would probably have been unacceptable anyway. For she had come alone, not accompanied by a male family member into a house where only men were present. This unacceptable behavior could not be tolerated by a Pharisee or by anyone else in first-century Palestinian Jewish society.

We can presume, then, that it required some effort for the woman to enter the house. Why had she been so persistent about making personal contact with Jesus? Luke does not tell us. Unlike the woman with the flow of blood, this woman had no illness from which she was seeking a cure. She was not a relative of Jesus' or of the Pharisee's. In this strange story, Jesus seems more like a rock star and the woman like a groupie.

She gains entrance to the house with her alabaster jar of ointment. Both the jar and the ointment would have been quite valuable. She says nothing at all. Without words she anoints his feet. Crying, she lets her tears fall on his feet and dries them with her hair, while continuing to kiss his feet and anoint them. Simon the Pharisee apparently knows the woman, or at least knows of her. He knows that she is a sinner. He knows that by touching Jesus she is rendering Jesus ritually impure. Luke then treats us to a brief interior monologue of the Pharisee, "If this man were a prophet, he would have known who and what kind of woman this is who is touching him—that she is a sinner" (7:39).

Jesus then tells Simon a simple parable about a creditor and two debtors. One debtor owed five-hundred denarii; the other fifty. The creditor canceled both debts. Jesus then asks Simon which of the debtors will love the creditor more. He answers, "I suppose the one for whom he canceled the greater debt" (Luke 7:43). Jesus affirms his answer and then makes a startling comparison between Simon and the woman:

> "Do you see this woman? I entered your house; you gave me no water for my feet, but she has bathed my feet with her tears and dried them with her hair. You gave me no kiss, but from the time I came in she has not stopped kissing my feet. You did not anoint my head with oil, but she has anointed my feet with ointment. Therefore, I tell you, her sins, which were many, have been forgiven; hence she has shown great love. But the one to whom little is forgiven, loves little" (7:44–47).

Jesus then tells the woman that her sins are forgiven, that her faith has saved her, and that she may go in peace.

To this point we have been under the impression that Simon and Jesus were alone with the woman. Luke now tells us that others were with them at the table, and these others complain about Jesus claiming the authority to forgive sins.

The story tells us quite a bit about Jesus and his relationships with and understanding of women. First, it reiterates that Jesus does not care about Jewish ritual purity laws. These laws, of foremost concern for the Pharisee, make him think that Jesus is no real prophet because he should have known that the woman was a sinner and should not touch him. Simon cannot imagine that Jesus would have wanted to be touched by a ritually impure person. When Jesus reveals his awareness that the woman is a sinner and yet is pleased that she has touched him, Simon must have been shocked. He knows that Jesus understands the ritual purity laws, yet he sees Jesus flagrantly violating them. Furthermore, he doubtless saw this woman's whole display of kissing Jesus' feet, crying, and drying Jesus' feet with her hair as offensive to all moral propriety. Her actions gave every appearance of being improper sexual advances toward Jesus. Not only was she a sinner, she was in the very process of sinning.

Second, Jesus recognizes that the woman is expressing her genuine love for him. He accepts love from whomever gives it, regardless of gender, religious purity, or ethnicity. Simon the Pharisee, who is the right gender, is the right ethnicity, and is religiously pure, offers Jesus no indication of love.

Third, Jesus forgives both the woman and Simon of their sins, though neither of them has asked for his forgiveness. The woman, knowing her need for much forgiveness, loved Jesus more. Simon, a righteous Pharisee, had less need for forgiveness, at least by Old Testament law. He loved Jesus less.

The story is quite typical of the behavior of Jesus. He prefers sinners to the righteous. He welcomes the presence of women. What Simon sees as the incorrect and inappropriate behavior of the woman does not embarrass Jesus. Jesus is concerned only with the intention of her actions, not with how well they conform to the etiquette of the day. He sees her as a person of love, and a person of love is a person of God. The Pharisee is a person of standards and rules. In his own understanding, his standards and rules make him a person of God. Jesus challenges this understanding. Luke concludes the story with regard to the woman. She goes away with the assurance of forgiveness, salvation, and the authentication of her own self-worth within a society that does not value her.

Luke does not conclude the story with regard to Simon the Pharisee. Does Simon come then or at some later point to understand the message of Jesus and of the woman, or does he continue blindly and uncritically to follow the ways of his tradition? Most of us are the Simons of the story. We want to live by the rules, and we feel disdain for those who do not. Jesus challenges our view. Will we come to understand his message?

MARY MAGDALENE

She was the last person at the cross. She was the first person at the tomb. No follower of Jesus was more faithful. Yet we know remarkably little about her. Later Christian tradition would embellish her character in ways that have nothing to do with what we know historically about her. To this day the majority of Christians, when asked about her, would say that she was a former prostitute who became a follower of Jesus. Yet nothing in any of the Gospels indicates that she had ever been a prostitute or in any way a woman of questionable morality. Perhaps it would be best for us to look at exactly what the Gospels do say about her.

Mary Magdalene is mentioned, though briefly, in all the Gospels. Although the empty tomb stories in the four Gospels are at great variance with one another, one thing on which they all agree is that Mary Magdalene was at the tomb of Jesus on the day of resurrection before any of his male disciples were there. Beyond this, little bits of information can be gleaned about her from the individual Gospels.

In Luke 8:1–2 we read, "The twelve were with him, as well as some women who had been cured of evil sprits and infirmities: Mary, called Magdalene, from whom seven demons had gone out." This description of her is echoed in the longer ending of Mark (16:9). These verses contain two pieces of information about her.

First, she was from the village of Magdala. Magdalene is not a family name; rather, it denotes her place of origin. Magdala was a small village less than halfway up the steep hillside on the northwest corner of the Sea of Galilee. Excavations of the village conducted from 1971 through 1973 revealed it to be a very small village with a small but well-constructed synagogue. During the lifetime of Jesus, it was an all-Jewish village. Its name is Aramaic, which is doubtless the language that was spoken there. Fishing was the primary occupation of its inhabitants. The views from Magdala are spectacular. Below and to the left, one sees the town of Capernaum, the hometown of Peter and Andrew and of a considerably larger synagogue. Up to the left, one sees the magnificent vista of the Golan Heights. Far down to the right, one can see the city of Tiberias, a Greco-Roman city under construction during the lifetime of Jesus. On a clear day one can see all the way to the south end of the Sea of Galilee, where it empties into the onflowing Jordan River. It was an ordinary Jewish village, distinguished only by the extraordinary beauty of the views its residents beheld every day.

The other thing Luke's text tells us is that "seven demons had gone out" of Mary Magdalene. Although Luke's text does not specifically say that Jesus had cast out the demons, that seems to be the assumption. Whether we understand demons in a literal sense or think of them symbolically as symptoms of mental illness, one thing is clear: Mary was mentally deranged before she met Jesus, and he restored her to full mental health. It is noteworthy that in the Gospels of Matthew, Mark, and Luke (though not in John), Jesus performs numerous demon exorcisms. They are almost as frequent as physical healings. Jesus was just as concerned with mental health as with physical health.

Mary knew that she owed her mental health to Jesus. Whatever mental demons had been tormenting her, they were now gone. She owed so much to him that she became his most loyal follower. Her loyalty has led to speculation over the centuries that they may have had some sort of romantic relationship. The brilliant Greek novelist Nikos Kanzantzakis, in his unjustly vilified novel *The Last Temptation of Christ,* deals with this speculation in a fascinating way. Too many people have seen the movie and not read the vastly superior book. Too many people have neither seen the movie nor read the book, and damned both out of ignorance. In the novel, Jesus has a dream while he is dying on the cross. In the dream he accepts the taunts of the passersby, "If you are the Son of God, come down from the cross." (Matt. 27:40). He comes down from the cross in another body, leaving his dead body on the cross. He takes Mary Magdalene, goes back to Galilee, marries her, and leads a normal life with a job and a family. The "last temptation of Christ" was to lead a normal life. But his normal life of wife and family was only a dream. Jesus denies the temptation and dies on the cross.

Another speculation of a romantic relationship between Jesus and Mary comes in the Andrew Lloyd Webber and Tim Rice musical *Jesus Christ Superstar.* The most poignant moment in the musical is when Mary Magdalene sings "I Don't Know How to Love Him." I suspect that the song fairly accurately portrays the feelings of the historical Mary Magdalene. She owed so much to him. She was so loyal to him; and he to her. Surely at some point, probably at many points, she wanted to marry him. In all her years of derangement, no man had ever shown her real love. The love she received from Jesus was a love she had never known before. How could she best love him back? Could she move from being a loyal follower to being a loving wife? Surely she must have thought about it. Could Jesus have ever thought about it?

In the college New Testament classes I have taught during the last quarter-century, I have always been interested to see the reactions of students at the suggestion of any sort of romantic expression by or toward Jesus. Virtually all students are surprised by the suggestion. It is something they have never thought of. Most are intrigued by the possibility. Some are appalled. For them the idea of any sort of romantic or sexual feeling toward or by Jesus is close to blasphemy. For them Jesus is the paragon of celibacy, utterly incapable of any romantic or sexual feelings and incapable of evoking any such feelings in others. They want a barely human Jesus. They want a Jesus who could feel pain, but not one who could feel pleasure. They can believe that Jesus wept, but not that he laughed. They can believe that Jesus turned water into wine, but not that he drank it. They can believe in Jesus and the pains, but not in Jesus and the pleasures.

Jesus died young. At thirty-three he was in the prime of life. What might have happened if the Romans had not crucified him on that dreadful day in the year 30? What if he had lived a long, full life? Playing the game of "hypothetical history" is risky. But it is clear that Jesus affirmed life in all its fullness. He enjoyed every act of pleasure that his life permitted him. Is it not strange that so many of Jesus' followers cannot conceive of the idea that Jesus could ever love any woman in the same way that I love my wife? Had Jesus lived beyond the age of thirty-three, Mary Magdalene might have become that special woman for him. But it was not to be. She saw him die, but that was not the last time she saw him. In his resurrection appearance to her in the Gospel of John, she has to let go of whatever hopes she may have had for a future relationship with him on earth. He says to her, "Do not hold on to me, because I have not yet ascended to the Father" (20:17). She has to let him go. He once was fully and completely human and in all ways full of life. Now she could know him only in spirit and memory. But spirit and memory were more than enough. In his last words to her, he told her to go and tell the disciples that he was ascending to the Father. When she found them, she said, "I have seen the Lord" (20:18). She thus became the first person to proclaim the risen Christ. She was the first evangelist.

THE WOMEN IN JESUS' LIFE

The Gospels are replete with stories of the women in Jesus' life. From the first Mary, who gave him birth, to the last Mary, who proclaimed his resurrection, women loved him, and he loved them in return.

The Gospel writers, all male, undoubtedly underplay the significance of women in Jesus' life. There is, to be sure, some variation among the Gospel writers. The women in Jesus' life are more significant to Luke than to any other Gospel writer. John would come in second in this regard; Mark and Matthew, a distant third and fourth. Even so, the role of women in Jesus' life comes clearly through all of them. Mary of Bethany and her sister Martha, Joanna, Salome, the woman at the well in Samaria, the "sinner" who anointed his feet, and many others were all important to him. He reveled in the pleasure of their company. He treated them equally with men. His expectations for them were no different from his expectations for his male disciples. For whatever reasons, his male disciples had abandoned him at the cross. The women stayed at his cross until the end. The women were the first ones to the tomb at his new beginning.

THE CHRISTIAN CHURCH AND WOMEN

In the earliest days of Christianity, the Church understood Jesus' message about women. Women held positions of leadership in the churches, served as apostles and prophets, and enjoyed a position of equality that they found nowhere else in Judaism or in Greco-Roman society.

The earliest Christian writer, Paul of Tarsus, cites numerous examples of this equality. In Romans 16:1 Paul commends Phoebe, the minister of the church at Cenchreae, a few miles south of Rome. Some English translations of the Bible attempt to cover up the leadership role of Phoebe by translating the Greek word for *minister* as something else. The Revised Standard Version translates it *deaconess,* even though the word has the same masculine gender ending as when it is used for male ministers. The New Revised Standard Version translates it *deacon.* On three other occasions, the exact same Greek word is used as a title for a male (Eph. 6:21; Col. 1:7, 4:7); in those places it is translated *minister.* We should note that the NRSV provides a footnote in reference to Phoebe, offering the alternative translation *or minister* for Romans 16:1. But when the same Greek word is used for a man, it is translated *minister* in the text, not in a footnote. The NRSV, however, does better than the New International Version, which translates the word as *minister* when it applies to a man, but as *servant* when it refers to Phoebe.

Besides ministers, the most important offices in the earliest churches were apostles and prophets. We mentioned earlier the female apostle Junia. Paul also speaks of women prophets in the churches. In 1 Corinthians 11:5 he says that the Corinthian women prophets should wear coverings on their heads. In Acts 21:8–9 we read that Philip the evangelist had four unmarried daughters who were prophets.

In one of the most powerful verses in the entire New Testament, Paul proclaims the total equality of all people: "There is no longer Jew or Greek, there is no longer slave or free, there is no longer male and female; for all of you are one in Christ Jesus" (Gal. 3:28). In a society in which virtually all relationships were conceived in hierarchical terms, Paul's statement in this verse must have been truly shocking to his earliest readers.

As wonderful as Christian gender equality was, it did not last long. Anti-Christian Romans specifically accused the early Christian Church of being dominated by women, and therefore being something in which no self-respecting Roman would want to be involved. By the end of the first century, the Christian Church had thoroughly accommodated itself to the dominant Roman culture by systematically excluding women from positions of authority within the Church. A pseudo-Paulinist would write a letter in Paul's name saying that women are not permitted to speak in church or have authority over men (1 Tim. 2:11–15). Virtually all New Testament scholars agree that the First Letter to Timothy, along with the Second Letter to Timothy and Titus, the so-called pastoral epistles, were not written by Paul but by a later follower who was writing in his name. A shorter version of this statement was later inserted by a manuscript copyist into a copy of Paul's First Letter to the Corinthians (14:34–36), from which it was recopied by almost all subsequent manuscript copyists. Nothing could be further from the thinking of the Apostle Paul, who shows us in so many places in his authentic letters that women were in positions of authority in the early Church.

Once women were excluded from positions of authority in the Church, their status was further reduced within Christianity by centuries of misogynistic Church fathers, whose writings continually deprecated and demeaned women. Subsequent centuries, all the way down to our own, have witnessed the Christian Church's continued abuse of Jesus' understanding of women. Although most of the mainline Protestant denominations have moved to full equality for women, the Roman Catholic, Eastern Orthodox, Mormon, and Southern Baptist Churches still deny Christian equality, the most basic ethical principle for which Jesus stood.

My minister's name is Susan. She embodies for our congregation all the virtues of those New Testament women who followed Jesus and faithfully led the Church, who were last at the cross and first at the tomb.

5 / JESUS AND SONG

Song is as old as the human species. Our prehistoric ancestors were singing wordlessly before they learned coherent speech. In all human cultures, the ear and brain attune themselves to the music the culture develops. The more learned and sophisticated the culture becomes, the more complex and varied its music.

The Bible is filled with music. Many scholars think that the earliest piece of biblical literature is the "Song of Miriam" (Exod. 15:21). Other pieces of biblical literature considered to be among the most ancient are also songs: the "Song of Deborah" in Judges, chapter 5, and the "Song of Moses" in Exodus, chapter 15. The songs, composed shortly after the events they portray, were passed down through the oral tradition for many generations before they reached written form in our biblical texts. The accompanying prose accounts in Exodus, chapter 14, and Judges, chapter 4, were written after the songs were composed and are based in large measure on the songs. Indeed, if it were not for the songs, we would probably know nothing of the ancient events they portray.

A relatively recent American event parallels and demonstrates this ancient Hebrew phenomenon. In 1976 a ship named the *Edmund Fitzgerald* sank in a storm on Lake Superior. Few Americans outside the region of the Upper Midwest would know of this event if the popular singer Gordon Lightfoot had not written a song about it. The song, "The Wreck of the *Edmund Fitzgerald*," far more than any newspaper, magazine, or TV news account, has preserved the memory of that tragic event.

THE PSALMS

Singing became an early and important aspect of Hebrew worship. The Book of Psalms in the Hebrew Scriptures was the hymnbook of the early Jews and, later, of the early Christians. We have the words of the 150 psalms in the Psalter, we have names for the tunes for many of them, and we have names and descriptions of the musical instruments used in antiquity, but we do not know how this ancient music sounded. Humans began to write as early as 3000 B.C.E., but we did not devise a means of musical notation for another three-and-a-half millennia. We have scarcely any surviving texts of musical notation from before 1000 C.E. Despite these difficulties, the Psalms tell us quite a lot about song in ancient Israel.

The Psalter comprises several distinct types of psalms. Scholars usually divide them into four types: lament psalms, thanksgiving psalms, royal psalms, and hymns. The lament psalms are probably our least favorite today. To our present-day preferences and sensibilities, the laments of the psalmists may seem almost paranoid. The college students I teach are inclined to refer to these psalmists as "whiners." Psalm 59 is a good example:

> Deliver me from my enemies, O my God;
> protect me from those who rise up against me.
> Deliver me from those who work evil;
>   from the bloodthirsty save me.
>
> Even now they lie in wait for my life;
> the mighty stir up strife against me.
> For no transgression or sin of mine, O Lord,
> for no fault of mine, they run and make ready (1–4).

Before we start feeling too negatively about the melodrama of the individual laments, we should realize their value in times of crisis and trouble. In the weeks after the destruction of the World Trade Center, on September 11, 2001, I found the paranoia of the lament psalms far less disturbing than I did before that ignominious day. As I read them now, they give some comfort that they did not give before. While I was watching a National Football League pregame show on television, before the first games played after September 11, I heard one of the sportscasters speak specifically of Psalm 10, one of the lament psalms, as having brought him comfort during this difficult time.

Like us, Jesus lived in troubled times. The oppressive Roman military force that occupied and ruled his native land would eventually bring him to his terrible death on the cross. While he hung in agony on that cross, Jesus remembered and quoted, perhaps even sadly sang, the first line of a very sad lament: "My God, my God, why have you forsaken me?" (Ps. 22:1).

The whining and groaning and moaning of the lament psalms is never all that there is to them. All the lament psalms also contain, and usually end with, words of praise to God. No matter how bad the psalmist's situation may be, he or she can still praise God, can still experience the presence and even the glory of God in the midst of life's most terrible situations.

When from the cross Jesus sang the first line of Psalm 22, I think that he had the entire psalm in mind. If I were to say the more familiar first line, "The LORD is my shepherd," which comes from the very next psalm in the Psalter, I think almost every reader of this book would know the lines that follow. Jesus knew the Psalter better than we do. He quoted the first line of Psalm 22 because the whole psalm spoke so clearly to the situation in which he found himself on the cross. Without speaking them, he certainly remembered these lines:

> A company of evildoers encircles me.
> My hands and feet have shriveled;
> I can count all my bones.
> They stare and gloat over me;
> they divide my clothes among themselves,
> and for my clothing they cast lots (Ps. 22:16–18).

Some versions translate the second line above as, "They have pierced my hands and feet." The Hebrew is uncertain here, and probably the NRSV translation ("My hands and feet have shriveled") is more accurate. Even so, we can readily see how Jesus' situation called this psalm to his mind. When he quoted its first line, he had the whole psalm in mind. Like so many other lament psalms, this one begins in sorrow but ends in praise:

> All the ends of the earth shall remember
> and turn to the Lord;
> And all the families of the nations
> shall worship before him.
> For dominion belongs to the Lord,
> and he rules over the nations. . . .
>
> Posterity will serve him;
> future generations will be told about the Lord,
> and proclaim his deliverance to a people yet unborn,
> saying that he has done it (Ps. 22:27–28,30–31).

Although Jesus experienced true agony and despair on the cross, the words he spoke were not his own, but those of the psalm. Christians who have been troubled by his words on the cross need to read Psalm 22 in full to know that even in the midst of his deepest suffering, Jesus could still praise God.

If times in America are as troubled when you are reading this as they are while I am writing it, you might find comfort in some of the community lament psalms, which often are laments for the entire nation of ancient Israel. Some of the communal laments are Psalms 44, 74, 79, 80, and 83. The entire Old Testament Book of Lamentations is a communal lament over the destruction of Jerusalem by the Babylonians in 586 B.C.E. Individual laments include Psalms 3, 5, 7, 11, 31, 51, 69, 88, 109, and 130.

Thanksgiving psalms convey a mood totally different from the laments. They are positive, upbeat, and grateful, often thanking God for specific things God has done in the life of the psalmist or the community. Examples include Psalms 30, 34, 92, and 116, all of which may have been used in the liturgical setting at the time the offering was made in Hebrew worship. Psalm 107 is a great example, with a strong refrain (the last two lines of this excerpt) that is repeated again and again:

> O give thanks to the Lord, for he is good;
> for his steadfast love endures forever. . . .
>
> Some wandered in desert wastes,
> finding no way to an inhabited town;

hungry and thirsty,
their soul fainted within them.
Then they cried to the Lord in their trouble,
and he delivered them from their distress;
he led them by a straight way,
until they reached an inhabited town.
Let them thank the Lord for his steadfast love,
for his wonderful works to humankind (Ps. 107:1,4–8).

Royal psalms appear to have had their original settings not in worship but in events at the court of the king. The most obvious example is Psalm 45, in which the psalmist states, "I address my verses to the king" (v. 1). Other royal psalms give thanks to God for military victories, as did those earliest songs in the Hebrew Bible. Examples include Psalms 18, 20, and 21.

The fourth type, the hymns, is the most important for us today. Like our modern hymns, many of which are based on the psalms, these hymns were composed for use in worship and written to be sung. More than any of the other psalms, they tell us about ancient Hebrew music and its use in worship. Perhaps the most familiar of these is Psalm 100, which begins:

Make a joyful noise to the Lord, all the earth.
Worship the Lord with gladness;
Come into his presence with singing (1–2).

Psalm 95, which contains a number of the same words, gives a more detailed picture of Hebrew worship:

O come, let us sing to the Lord;
let us make a joyful noise to the rock of our salvation!
Let us come into his presence with thanksgiving;
let us make a joyful noise to him with songs of praise! . . .

O come, let us worship and bow down,
let us kneel before the Lord, our Maker! (1–2, 6)

Psalm 47 lets us know that the Hebrew people were not averse to loud praise in worship, with clapping and shouting: "Clap your hands, all you peoples; / shout to God with loud songs of joy" (v. 1).

Some of the psalms are a mixture of types. Psalm 42, for example, is a lament, perhaps the most beautiful lament in the entire Psalter. In the midst of the lament, the psalmist remembers better days, and what he remembers particularly is the joy of Hebrew worship:

As a deer longs for flowing streams,
so my soul longs for you, O God.
My soul thirsts for God,
for the living God.
When shall I come and behold
the face of God?
My tears have been my food
day and night,
while people say to me continually,
"Where is your God?"

These things I remember,
as I pour out my soul:
how I went with the throng,
and led them in procession to the house of God,
with glad shouts and songs of thanksgiving,
a multitude keeping festival.

Why are you cast down, O my soul,
and why are you disquieted within me?
Hope in God; for I shall again praise him,
my help and my God (1–5).

Most of the psalms have superscriptions that are not a part of the psalm itself. Some of the superscriptions say nothing more than "Of David." For other psalms, the superscriptions provide a historical or literary context. Still other superscriptions give specific instructions to the leader or choirmaster about the tune to which the psalm is to be sung, information about accompanying musical instruments or knowledge of the literary genre in which the psalm is written. The elaborate superscription of Psalm 56 offers several types of information: "To the leader: according to The Dove on Far-off Terebinths. Of David. A Miktam, when the Philistines seized him in Gath."

The name of the tune is "The Dove on Far-off Terebinths." "Of David" refers to the composer of the psalm, or the school that grew up around him and continued after his death. A "Miktam" is the literary genre of the psalm. "When the Philistines seized him in Gath" indicates the historical or literary context of the First Book of Samuel, chapter 27. These instructions imparted much information to the ancient Hebrew choirmaster, but they tell *us* far less. We do not know what a Miktam is, other than that it is a literary genre. Though we have the name of the tune, we have no idea what the tune sounded like. We do learn from the superscriptions that set tunes could be sung to the words of more than one psalm.

In addition to the superscriptions, we have one musical direction that occurs within the psalms themselves. It is the Hebrew word *selah,* the exact meaning of which we do not know. In Psalm 88, for example, the word occurs twice, at the end of verse 7 and at the end of verse 10. It is most likely a direction for an instrumental flourish to be played after those particular verses are sung.

The Psalter ends with five psalms of praise. Each of these begins with the phrase "Praise the LORD," which translates from the Hebrew *Hallelu-jah.* The last psalm is the most musical of all:

> Praise the Lord!
> Praise God in his sanctuary;
> praise him in his mighty firmament!
> Praise him for his mighty deeds;
> praise him according to his surpassing greatness!
>
> Praise him with trumpet sound;
> praise him with lute and harp!
> Praise him with tambourine and dance;
> praise him with strings and pipe!
> Praise him with clanging symbols;
> praise him with loud clashing symbols!
> Let everything that breathes praise the Lord!
> Praise the Lord! (1–6)

This psalm is a musical masterpiece—how wonderful it would be to hear it sung to its original tune. The psalm builds to a crescendo with the rapid repetition of the phrase *Hallelu-hu* ("Praise him") at the beginning of each line after the first two lines. The effect is hypnotic and compelling. The music gets louder as the progression of instruments gets louder, culminating with "loud clashing cymbals." But even this is not enough. The penultimate line is the ultimate praise, "Let everything that breathes praise the LORD!"

All this demonstrates that the ancient Hebrews had an elaborate, sophisticated, and well-developed musical system that brought order and meaning to their worship of God and joy to their lives. The sound of musical instruments, as indicated in Psalm 150, combined with the singing of the people, must have been powerful indeed. Psalm 150 also indicates that the people danced during worship. Dancing is a logical and pleasurable outcome of singing. The rhythms of music make us want to move, and the ancient Hebrews did not resist the urge to dance while praising God.

We cannot be sure how much of this musical system survived to the time of Jesus. We can be sure, though, that when Jesus went to the temple in Jerusalem, he heard and very likely sang the music of the Book of Psalms. We can imagine that these same tunes and others were on his lips and in his mind and heart as he traveled and ministered throughout the region of the Galilee.

THE SONG OF SONGS

The Psalms were, for the most part, used in the public worship of God, but another song in the Hebrew Scriptures is an utterly secular love song. It is the song attributed to King Solomon, and it is perhaps the most beautiful love poetry ever written. Though commonly called the Song of Solomon today, the grammar of the song's original title, the Song of Songs, tells us something about how it was regarded by those who passed it from generation to generation.

The Hebrew language lacks comparative and superlative forms of adjectives. In English we make the comparative form of an adjective, such as *strong*, by putting an *er* at the end of the word: The eagle is strong*er* than the sparrow. We make the superlative form of the adjective by adding *est* to show that a particular noun displays the highest degree of the quality the adjective describes: "That was the sweet*est* pie I have ever eaten." Because Hebrew lacks these forms, it has to find other ways to express comparatives and superlatives. One way is to repeat the noun in what is called the construct form. This is expressed in English with the word *of*. The phrase *song of songs* thus means "the most superlative song," "the greatest song," or "the most beautiful song."

It is interesting that the ancient Hebrews would have considered this secular poem about the sexual love of a man and a woman to be the greatest song, but so they titled it. Perhaps they already knew what more than two thousand years of subsequent songwriting would bear out—that romantic love is, far more often than anything else, the theme of songs.

We have already discussed the Song of Songs in some detail in the chapter on Jesus and wine. Here I want only to point out some musical qualities of the Song of Songs. Though we think of it as a poem, it is exactly what it says it is—a song. It is to be sure an extended song, with different dramatic parts: a male soloist, a female soloist, and a chorus. It is more like a scene from an opera or a musical than a song. Certainly it was sung, though as with all other ancient music, we cannot know what it sounded like.

The Song of Songs may well have been performed at wedding feasts. It would certainly not have been sung at worship services. Might it have been sung at the wedding feast at Cana, where Jesus was present? Would Jesus have known its beautiful love lyrics? While the Gospels never show Jesus quoting from the Song of Songs, they do consistently show him quoting from the Hebrew Scriptures. That he knew the scriptures so well in general is good evidence that he knew the Song of Songs in particular. Like the Psalms, its lyrics may have been on his lips as he walked from one village to another throughout the region of Galilee.

We cannot know what Jesus felt or thought about anything except to the extent that the Gospels tell us. We have a good idea of how Jesus understood his mission after his baptism, but we have little idea of how he understood himself. We do know, from the Gospels, that Jesus was fully human. Our conventional picture of a sexless Jesus, Jesus the monk, in all probability does not correspond to reality. Although we have no evidence that Jesus ever married or had a romantic relationship, it seems altogether possible that he thought about it. It seems altogether possible that he could have longed to meet a special someone with whom to enjoy the pleasures of human love for the rest of his life. Such thoughts may have come to him as he crossed the verdant Galilean hills in springtime. The beauty of nature around him could have called to his mind verses from the Song of Songs that he had likely learned in his youth:

"Arise, my love, my fair one,
and come away;
for now the winter is past,
the rain is over and gone.
The flowers appear on the earth;
the time of singing has come,
and the voice of the turtledove
is heard in our land.
The fig tree puts forth its figs,
and the vines are in blossom;

they give forth fragrance.
Arise, my love, my fair one,
and come away.
O my dove, in the clefts of the rock,
in the covert of the cliff,
let me see your face,
let me hear your voice;
for your voice is sweet,
and your face is lovely (2:10–14).

Though his last days would be a time of strife and sadness, Jesus would remember better times in earlier days, days in the Galilean spring, when "the time of singing" had come.

JESUS AND SONG IN THE GOSPELS

Although the Gospels provide rich source material for Christian hymns and songs, they are remarkably bereft of song within themselves. They never refer specifically to Jesus singing or playing a musical instrument. Even the story that inspires more songs than any other, Luke's nativity story, contains no actual singing. The "Magnificat" of Mary, in Luke 1:46–55, which J. S. Bach would fashion into one of the greatest musical works of all time, was, according the text, spoken rather than sung. The "Song of Simeon," in Luke 2:29–32, is prefaced with, "Simeon took him [the baby Jesus] into his arms and praised God, saying . . ." (v. 28). Although praising God is associated with singing, Luke writes that Simeon was not singing but saying the words that would ever after be associated with him. Even the angelic voices heard by the shepherds at the time of the first Christmas spoke, rather than sang, those famous words that have been sung ever since, *Gloria in excelsis deo*: "Glory to God in the highest heaven, / and on earth peace among those whom he favors!" (Luke 2:14).

Though Jesus surely sang, and I suspect sang well and often, the Gospels record only one instance of it—with his disciples on the night before his crucifixion. It happened immediately after Jesus and the disciples had eaten the bread and wine of the last supper in an upper room in Jerusalem: "When they had sung the hymn, they went out to the Mount of Olives" (Mark 14:26; also Matt. 26:30). Because the reference is to *the* hymn rather than *a* hymn, it was surely the hymn that ended the Jewish Passover ritual that Jesus and the disciples were keeping that night.

The Gospels contain few other musical references. One occurs in Jesus' parable of the prodigal son in Luke, chapter 15. After the prodigal returns home from his profligate sojourn in a distant country, his father kills the fatted calf for a great celebration. The elder brother, the one who had never left but had faithfully worked on his father's land, was returning from the field. "When he came and approached the house, he heard music and dancing" (15:25). The dour elder brother did not appreciate the celebration, and voiced his complaint to the father. In the end of the story, the father consoles him and tries to get him to understand with this explanation: "Son, you are always with me, and all that is mine is yours. But we had to celebrate and rejoice, because this brother of yours was dead and has come to life; he was lost and has been found" (15:31–32).

That is the end of the story. We are left to imagine whether the elder brother did come to understand and whether he was ever reconciled with his father and his brother.

The parable of the prodigal son may be the most popular of Jesus' parables. I suspect, though, that as many times as we have heard it read and preached, we have never thought about the music and dance in it. What is a very minor element in the story is our major consideration in this chapter. We read the story with mixed emotions. Many American Christians, particularly those of a more evangelical mindset, identify readily with the prodigal. Many who had dramatic conversion experiences know what it is like to have been lost and to now be found. Their own experience resonates clearly with that most popular of hymns, "Amazing Grace." On the other hand, some of us who have spent our entire lives in the Church may feel a little differently about the story. We may have a lot of sympathy for the elder brother. Like the elder brother, we have lived our entire lives trying to be faithful to our Father. We have never gone off the deep end, never plunged into the abyss of faithless living. We have never needed to be rescued from a slough of decadence of our own making. Like the elder brother, we harbor a bit of resentment toward the dramatically converted. We think that we deserve better treatment. We are not so eager to dance at their celebration. In this parable Jesus speaks a word against us. He leaves the story open as to whether the elder brother will join in the celebration. Will we?

The celebration is complete with music and dance. Jesus never displayed any consternation about dancing, or, as we saw in the story of the wedding feast at Cana, drinking. The wild and free celebration for the return of the prodigal meets with Jesus' complete approval. He calls us to join the celebration, to eat the fatted calf, to drink the water made wine, to dance to the music of life.

Jesus speaks of music and dance in only one other passage. It comes in the context of Jesus comparing himself to John the Baptist. We have looked at this passage in our examination of wine. We will look at it here from a different angle:

> "To what can I compare this generation? They are like children sitting in the marketplaces and calling out to others:
> 'We played the flute for you,
> and you did not dance;
> we sang a dirge,
> and you did not mourn.'
> For John came neither eating nor drinking, and they say, 'He has a demon.' The Son of Man came eating and drinking, and they say, 'Here is a glutton and a drunkard, a friend of tax collectors and "sinners."'" (Matt. 11:16–19, NIV; see also Luke 7:31–35)

It is not an easy passage to understand. A scan of biblical commentaries will turn up a variety of interpretations. The interpretation I offer here, with its focus on music, will be different from any others we are likely to read or hear.

Jesus illustrates the difference between himself and John the Baptist with a two-line riddle about children playing musical games. There are two groups of children, those who want to play and those who do not. Those who want to play first offer fun music, the music of flutes, to dance to. The other group refuses to join in the dance. Those who want to play then offer a game with the opposite kind of music, a dirge to which the group can play a mock funeral game with feigned mourning. The other group will not join in this game either.

Jesus then compares the two kinds of music to himself and John. The happy dance music of the flute is his. It represents all the joy of the message he brings of the Kingdom of God coming on earth. The Kingdom is characterized by love, joy, and peace. It sees all the good things in this life and joyously experiences them. It is a Kingdom of the here and now, which spreads the love, feels the joy, and creates the peace. Jesus calls on any who would follow him to join the Kingdom, to do those things that will bring the Kingdom to its fullness on earth, just as it already is in heaven. Those children who refuse to play are those who reject the Kingdom of God that Jesus presents. Not only do they reject the message of Jesus, they also reject the message of John the Baptist. Jesus pulled no punches in showing the sharp difference between his message and that of John the Baptist. The Gospels give us enough quotations from

John the Baptist to give us a good idea of what his message was; it was an apocalyptic message. John looked at the world negatively and saw it as a place of irredeemable evil. He looked for the world to end soon, in a fiery judgment of God. He called on all who heard him to repent in order to escape God's harsh judgment. "Even now the ax is lying at the root of the trees; every tree therefore that does not bear good fruit is cut down and thrown into the fire," John the Baptist said in Matthew 3:10.

Some New Testament scholars these days see Jesus as a faithful disciple of John the Baptist who carried on his apocalyptic message to the next generation. That Jesus did not see it this way is evident in the passage we are examining. Though he always shows respect for John the Baptist, he clearly demarcates his message from John's. That the disciples of John the Baptist continued to exist as a separate group from the followers of Jesus long after the deaths of both Jesus and John is further evidence of the sharp differences in their messages (see Acts 19:1–7).

The children in Jesus' riddle who refuse to join in the game in which they dance also refuse to join in the game in which they mourn. They will not play at all. They are like the people of Jesus' generation, specifically the Sadducees and the Pharisees, who rejected both John and Jesus. While Jesus would prefer that they receive his message, he would rather they accept the message of John the Baptist than receive no new message at all.

The difference in thinking between Jesus and John the Baptist roughly parallels the difference in thinking among major types of Christians today. Conservative evangelical and fundamentalist Christians, the fastest-growing group today, share the apocalyptic framework of John the Baptist. Revelation is their favorite book of the Bible. They look for signs in current events of the fulfillment of biblical prophecy. They do not read the Bible in its own historical context. They believe that the world is an evil place ruled by Satan, which will soon, indeed in their own lifetime, be destroyed by a vengeful God. They, the true Christians, will be "raptured," that is, taken up into heaven before the destruction begins.

This apocalyptic view eradicates the need for any sort of Christian social ethic. If the planet is soon to be destroyed, there is no point in doing anything to save it. Ecology and conservation are a waste of time and money. Any movement toward world peace is an illusion. They will staunchly oppose organizations that work toward world peace, such as the United Nations. Although these groups will not say so quite this directly, they are against world peace. For the second coming of Christ and the end to occur, the world needs to be in turmoil. At times of peace, they can regard it only as a false peace.

Such an understanding of God is derived primarily from Old Testament depictions of a God of vengeance who loves them but hates their enemies. Their enemies include anyone who is not an evangelical Christian, but especially liberals, feminists, and homosexuals. They also oppose the findings of modern science that run counter to a literalistic interpretation of the Genesis creation accounts.

Until the last two decades, these groups kept largely to themselves, had little involvement in American society, and even less in American politics. Then they discovered television. The television ministries of Jerry Falwell and Pat Robertson, among others, have gained huge followings. They have entered the political arena and have had some effect on public policy.

The growing power of apocalypticism is also made evident by the tremendous sales of the Left Behind series of futuristic novels. This series, which will eventually comprise twelve books, has already sold millions of copies. The first book in the series begins with the rapture of the true Christians. The first novel opens with the rapture—"true Christians" suddenly disappear from view. If one is an airplane pilot, his plane crashes, killing hundreds. The merciless God who causes this to happen remains remarkably aloof from the havoc wreaked. Instead, God allows an evil Romanian to become the head of the evil United Nations and to embark on a program of unmitigated evil.

It is a sad commentary on the current state of American religion that despite the abundance and availability of excellent Christian books and writers, these theologically weak, morally deficient, and literarily inferior books are the best sellers. It is a further sad commentary that their apocalyptic views are beginning to dominate the American religious landscape. Jesus plays the flute, but they do not dance. They sing a dirge, and their followers cry. Most Americans stand by and neither dance nor cry.

When conservative evangelicals think of Jesus, they think of the cross and the resurrection. Their theology is far more directly derived from the letters of Paul than from the Gospels. Jesus' teachings during his lifetime on earth get short shrift from these Christians.

Jesus invites us to dance. He plays for us the music of life. He loves the world; he sees it as a place of ultimate potential good. God, too, loves the world. In the creation story of Genesis 1:1—2:4, after each act of creation, the text says, "And God saw that it was good." After God creates men and women, too, "God saw everything that he had made, and indeed, it was very good" (Gen. 1:31). Sin subsequently comes into the world, and humanity needs salvation, but God's positive view of the world never changes. God wants not to destroy the world but to redeem it. Indeed, the most famous verse in the Bible begins, "For *God so loved the world* that he gave his only Son . . ." (John 3:16, emphasis added).

The teachings of Jesus in the Gospels consistently place the world, and the human beings who dwell in it, in a positive light. The central focus of the teaching of Jesus is *not* the imminent end of the world. Jesus never predicts his own physical return in the last days. The terms "second coming" and "rapture" occur nowhere in the Bible. The consistent focus of Jesus' preaching is the Kingdom of God (or in Matthew's terms, the kingdom of heaven; there is no difference in meaning). The Kingdom of God is the major topic of Jesus' parables. He never provides a blueprint for the Kingdom of God, but does give subtle inferences to help us understand what the Kingdom is. Consider these most basic Kingdom of God parables:

> [Jesus] also said, "With what can we compare the kingdom of God, or what parable will we use for it? It is like a mustard seed, which, when sown upon the ground, is the smallest of all the seeds on earth; yet when it is sown it grows up and becomes the greatest of all shrubs, and puts forth large branches, so that the birds of the air can make nests in its shade" (Mark 4:30–32).

The clear message of this parable is that the Kingdom of God starts small and grows to be very large. Jesus offers the same message with a different illustration in this short parable from Luke: "And again [Jesus] said, 'To what should I compare the Kingdom of God? It is like yeast that a woman took and mixed in with three measures of flour until all of it was leavened'" (13:20–21). In baking, yeast, though small in itself, is the ingredient that causes flat dough to rise into bread. The process is not immediate. It is slow enough that the baker does not actually see the bread rise, just as we do not see a mustard plant grow from a seed. We do not see the process happen. We see only the results of the process.

Once we see the Kingdom, we understand how valuable it is. The following Kingdom of God parables show its value:

> The kingdom of heaven is like treasure hidden in a field, which someone found and hid; then in his joy he goes and sells all that he has and buys that field.
>
> Again the Kingdom of Heaven is like a merchant in search of fine pearls; on finding one pearl of great value, he went and sold all that he had and bought it (Matt.13:44–46).

In other words, the Kingdom is here, but not everyone sees it. If you are not looking for it, you probably will not see it. But if you see it, you will recognize that it is more valuable than anything else. When is the Kingdom coming, and where will we see it? The Pharisees asked Jesus these very questions in Luke:

> Once Jesus was asked by the Pharisees when the kingdom of God was coming, and he answered, "The kingdom of God is not coming with things that can be observed, nor will they say, 'Look; here it is!' or 'There it is!' For, in fact, the kingdom of God is among you" (17:20–21).

The Kingdom of God is not going to come suddenly, instantly shattering all evil and restoring all good. The Kingdom of God is a process that has already begun. Jesus tells us that the Kingdom is already here; it is among us. We have only to see it and to join it. It is a seed that is growing. One day it will come into its fullness, not in a sudden burst, not in a massive destruction and replacement, but slowly, like a mustard plant. The Kingdom is already complete in its fullness in heaven. It will slowly come to fullness on earth. We pray for the Kingdom every time we pray the Lord's Prayer, "Thy Kingdom come, on earth, as it is in heaven." We participate in it when we sing at the prodigal's welcome-home party, when we dance to the flute that signals its presence in our midst.

THE MUSIC OF THE CHRISTIAN FAITH

From the time of the singing of that first Christian hymn at the Last Supper, until the singing of a billion voices in Christian hymns this past Sunday, song has been a mainstay of the faith. The entire Western musical tradition, from Gregorian chant to rock and roll, developed out of the Christian Church. Pope Gregory the Great inspired the process that eventuated in musical notation. Once music could be written down, it could be thoroughly preserved for future generations. The monks would sing their angelic chants day after day, century after century in performance of the central rite of Christian faith, the Holy Eucharist. In the High Middle Ages (the twelfth through the fifteenth centuries), a few individual composers would arise from the monasteries and convents to produce new chant, in notes that seemed at once to go up to heaven and come down from heaven. A French monk, Guillaume de

Machaut, composed music for the festivals of the Church, music that carried a cappella singing to new heights of beauty. A brilliant abbess of a convent in Germany, Hildegard von Bingen, wrote densely complex mystical literature and composed profoundly moving musical drama. The current revival of early music has seen the appearance of scores of recordings of her music during the last decade. I am listening now as I write to a recording of her chants called *Vision,* which sets her music with "new age" instrumentation. The effect is astonishing. This music, so ancient and mystical, becomes utterly modern and no less mystical. I was privileged to attend a performance of her mystical musical drama *Ordo Virtutum,* by the early music group Sequentia, in the great Gothic church that is Duke University Chapel. The experience was both profoundly religious and intensely musical. In her music I could hear the beginnings of those chords that in following centuries would crescendo to what is perhaps the greatest achievement of Western civilization, the classical symphonic and operatic tradition.

The great composers of the Church would arise over the course of the next few centuries: Palestrina, Pachelbel, Tallis, Purcell, Vivaldi, Handel, and pre-eminently, the greatest and most deeply religious of all composers, Johann Sebastian Bach.

What Shakespeare was to theater, Bach would become for music. His masses and motets, his cantatas and toccatas, his development of the form of the fugue, and his brilliantly contrived orchestral suites brought music to its pinnacle. His *Well-Tempered Clavier,* a set of forty-eight keyboard pieces, one for each key in the major-minor system, refined and defined the system of music that prevails in Western music to this day.

The organ had been used in churches for a couple of centuries when Bach became the first to fully recognize its potential as the king of instruments, the instrument that more than any other could convey in music the power and majesty of God. A massive church organ of eight or nine thousand pipes can produce eight or nine thousand distinctive sounds and imitate most of the instruments of an orchestra. Bach would use the organ to its fullest potential, ten fingers and two feet in full motion, producing a greater wealth of sound than human ears had ever heard. Only God could be more powerful.

For all his technical musical brilliance, Bach also had a theological acumen that gave full light to the depth of his faith. Yale historian Jaroslav Pelikan's book *Bach among the Theologians* shows how Bach profoundly matched his musical notes to the words of the liturgies handed down to him from centuries of the Church's worship. Perhaps no musical work is more profound than his B Minor Mass, and within it, no holier music was ever composed than the final

"Dona Nobis Pacem," or "Grant us peace." Here Bach transports us from earth to heaven and gives us an inspiring sense of the wonderful life that awaits us in the fullness of God's Kingdom.

Though Bach may represent the climax of the Western Christian musical crescendo, the tradition has continued with the wealth of two and a half more centuries of the greatest music human ears have ever heard. The music of the great ones went from the churches to the royal courts and beyond to the people. Every major European city, and soon every American city, would have concert halls and opera houses. The genius of the greatest genius, Wolfgang Amadeus Mozart, would be heard everywhere. Mozart wrote his first symphonies when he was five and six years old and his first opera when he was eleven. When he was eight, his father, Leopold, took him to a performance of an exceedingly complex twelve-part Tallis motet in St. Peter's Basilica in Rome. The Holy See treasured this music, and allowed no manuscripts of it to leave the cathedral, preventing it from being performed anywhere else. After the performance, Leopold told young Wolfgang about the Holy See's policy, so the child wrote down from memory all the notes of all the parts. The Vatican secret was no longer secret. Mozart wrote 626 major works by the time he died, far too young, at the age of 35, in 1791. Though most of his works are absolute music, that is to say, they have no programmatic aspect, tell no story, and evoke no specific images, he did write some religious music, the most important of which is his *Requiem,* his final work.

Other great European composers filled the nineteenth century with the lush and powerful chords of Romanticism. The vast majority of this music had its place outside the Church, yet even Beethoven wrote a *Missa Solemnis* (Solemn Mass), and Brahms wrote a profoundly spiritual *Requiem.* And Wagner, with his pagan inclinations, infused his grandly dramatic operas with religious ideas from half-Christian, half-pagan medieval tales like *Parsifal* and *Tristan and Iseult.*

An American in the late nineteenth century had an impact on music that went much further than anyone could have imagined. He did not compose a note. He did not sing or play any musical instruments. His only musical talent, like mine, was listening. Yet because of him, millions, perhaps billions of people the world over would be able to hear great music. His name was Thomas Edison. He invented, among many other things, the phonograph.

I once heard a recording that Johannes Brahms made in 1884 as a present to Thomas Edison. A somewhat scratchy but distinct voice came on that said in German-accented English, "Dr. Edison, this is Dr. Brahms, Johannes Brahms. I am going to play for you . . ." I do not remember the name of the work. It was a piano sonata, or at least a work that Brahms played on the piano. Edison's invention made possible not only the proliferation of classical music worldwide but also a profusion of all popular music forms from ragtime to rap.

Wagner developed the huge orchestras that enabled more expansive, complex, and variegated music than was previously possible. Composers like Mahler, Richard Strauss, Tchaikovsky, Rachmaninoff, and Stravinsky would bring into the early twentieth century the loudest, lushest, most extraordinary sounds the world had ever heard.

The twentieth century witnessed new and different styles of music. After the devastating impact of the First World War on Europe, the grand symphonies, operas, and ballets of the end of the late nineteenth century no longer seemed appropriate. Igor Stravinsky led the way with a new dissonance in music, a dissonance to which Western ears were not accustomed. At the premier performance of his shocking ballet *The Rite of Spring* in Paris in 1913, the normally open-minded French audience rioted, assaulting the orchestra with vegetables turned into missiles. The press accused Stravinsky of trying to destroy music as an art. Two years later the work played again in the same venue to audience ovation and rave reviews. The difficult, dissonant, enigmatic twentieth century had truly begun. The century produced greatness in the arts, but it was a greatness that was sometimes difficult to apprehend on first hearing.

The twentieth century would produce, with the help of developments in recording, more different kinds of music than any other century. The European classical tradition was well represented in the works of Sibelius, Rachmaninoff, Prokofiev, Elgar, and Vaughn Williams, among many, many others, including Americans Samuel Barber, Aaron Copland, and Leonard Bernstein. New twentieth-century dissonance appeared in the works of Stravinsky, Bartok, Janacek, and Shostakovich. Then came a totally different kind of music: from France, the impressionism of Debussy and Ravel; and from Italy, the music of Ottorino Respighi. This music used different tonal structures to convey impressions of the smaller things in life, things that the grand works of the romantics would not have considered worthy of a composition, such as "Moonlight," "Reflections on the Water," music about Botticelli paintings, and a slow, soft dance for a dead princess.

A Spanish school of composers would bring into classical music tone scales from the medieval Arab influences of the Moorish culture in Spain. Turina, deFalla, Albéniz, and Roderigo developed this music into a unique Spanish tradition that always stemmed, in one way or another, from the guitar. The blind Joaquin Roderigo, whose long life spanned almost the entire twentieth century, wrote a concerto for guitar and orchestra that has become probably the single most popular classical work of the century, the *Concerto de Aranjuez*.

Other composers, beginning with Arnold Schoenberg and including Webern, Berg, Stockhausen, and Cage, abandoned tonality altogether and produced works of extreme mathematical complexity and difficulty. Their works, considered so important by music critics in the mid-twentieth century, are rarely heard today.

Beyond music based on the classical tradition came a plethora of popular music styles. Today we hear jazz, pop, rock, country, new age, reggae, Celtic, and many other forms. All of these use the same tone scales, same musical systems, and same instruments (though some are now electrified) as the classical tradition. They are all outgrowths of Western classical music.

Unfortunately, the Western classical music tradition is in decline. The level of performance has never been greater, while the level of composition has rarely been worse. Atonal and serial music, with its total abandonment of the major-minor scale system, turned people away from the classical tradition. I remember the first symphony concert I went to on my own, apart from a school program. Pierre Boulez was conducting the BBC Symphony Orchestra. The entire first half of the program consisted of atonal music by Webern and Berg. More than two thirds of the audience left at intermission. They missed a performance of Debussy's wonderful *Le Jeux* in the second half. I wonder how many of those who left that concert in 1965 have never been to another symphony concert. Despite all the great tonal classical music that was written in the twentieth century, atonal music sent it all into decline.

Atonal music is rarely heard in concert or even on radio anymore. Current composers fall into the schools of minimalism, new romanticism, and spiritualism. While minimalists such as Philip Glass have provided a lot of movie music, and John Adams has written some interesting operas, it is the spiritualists, all writing from a basis in Christian belief, who are likely to have the longest lasting impact. The principal spiritualist composers are Henryk Górecki, Arvo Part, and John Tavener. Górecki's Symphony no. 3, *Symphony of Sorrowful Songs,* has become perhaps the most famous work of the movement. The entire work is slower than slow, a radical contrast to our fast-paced age and to the speed and volume of most popular music. The low strings play slowly and deeply to take us to a new depth in our own souls. A single soprano sings mournfully in Polish. One of the songs is a prayer written on the wall of a Nazi prison by a young mother with her baby. They did not survive the Holocaust. Górecki's symphony is deeply Christian, spiritual, and devoid of sentimentality and triteness.

John Tavener is an English composer who is perhaps best known for his "Song for Athene." It is one of the most remarkable pieces of music I know, and was heard around the world as the final work sung at the funeral of Princess Diana. Tavener composed the piece after the accidental death of a family friend. "Song for Athene" allows the hearer to mourn a death, gradually lifts the listener up to heaven with angelic voices of uncommon beauty, and then slowly allows us to return to earth, better off for the journey. Tavener is a convert to Russian Orthodox Christianity, and his music stems from his deep spirituality.

Perhaps the most popular composer of church music during the last two decades has been John Rutter, who was formerly the director of the King's College Choir at Cambridge University in England. Although he has written few congregational hymns, church choirs of all the mainline Protestant denominations regularly perform Rutter's many choral works. His "God Be in My Head" has become a mainstay among choir benedictions. His choral anthems are frequently heard in traditional worship services, and some consider his *Requiem* to be one of the great choral works of the twentieth century. The soft, mellifluous style of his music has had a tremendous influence on the development of much Christian music of the late twentieth century.

The single most popular composer of musical theater during the last three decades has been Andrew Lloyd Webber. Two of his best-known musicals, with lyrics by Tim Rice, have biblical sources. The first musical he wrote, *Joseph and the Amazing Technicolor Dreamcoat,* drew on the story of Joseph and his brothers. *Jesus Christ Superstar* depicts Christ's passion. The play, and the movie that followed it, are brilliantly conceived and offer a thought-provoking portrayal of Jesus. It is a loving Jesus, but one with a hard edge. Most of the music has a driving, pounding rock hardness that moves the narrative rapidly forward with potent dramatic tension. Though the libretto borrows from all the Gospels, the drama most closely resembles the account in the Gospel of Mark. In contrast to the more evenly paced Gospels of Matthew and Luke, and the at times slow-paced John, the Gospel of Mark is dramatic and intense. We know how the story of Jesus ends, but by reading it straight through in Mark or seeing it in *Superstar,* the speed of the narrative draws us in. Things happen quickly. The action tumbles us toward the cross with unstoppable momentum. Like Mark, *Superstar* ends without resurrection appearances (the earliest manuscripts of Mark lack resurrection appearances; they were added centuries later by dissatisfied copyists). The crucifixion is the climax. Everything points to it; everything leads to it. As many times as we have heard, read, or seen the story, we are still left in shock.

Andrew Lloyd Webber has written classical as well as show music. His *Requiem* was the best selling classical CD of 1992—a remarkable work in many ways. The first thing one notices about it in performance is that the symphony orchestra has no violins. Violins are normally the largest section of a symphony. With no violins, the effect of the other strings—violas, cellos, and basses—is striking. The predominance of lower strings gives the music a deeply somber quality that is appropriate to its theme.

The best-known and most beautiful part of the work is the *"Pie Jesu."* I think it is one of the most beautiful religious melodies written in the last century. It is a vocal duet, with two sopranos: one a boy, the other an adult female. The complexity of tone and overtone in the two identically pitched but differently colored voices is remarkable. The boy's voice is crystal clear and ethereal. The woman's voice is rich and earthy. The two together, singing simple Latin words of praise to Jesus, voice the incarnation—the heavenly Christ and the earthly Jesus in voices inextricably entwined in duet.

Sadly, the audiences for classical music are getting smaller and older. Despite reams of evidence that listening to and playing classical music is conducive to learning, it is all but vanishing in our public schools. Churches, the other great source of classical music, are now going over in droves to "contemporary worship," with tunes based too often in bland and clichéd pop music formats that make little impression on the heart, mind, and soul. New churches are being built without organs. Instead they have amplification systems and movie screens. Contemporary worship may develop further and improve, but at this point it has diminished the experience of traditional Christian worship.

It is ironic that in a day when classical music performance and recording are at their zenith, listening is in decline. Most Americans consider the music too complex, difficult, or stuffy. It takes some listening and some learning before the full pleasures of the music get through the mind and into the soul. When they finally do, the experience is incredibly and immensely enriching.

For the past two and a half years, I have organized and facilitated a small "Wine and Classical Music Group" with people from my church. We meet monthly at members' homes, and we socialize, eat hors d'oeuvres, taste wines, and listen to the music of a particular composer. The composer's music is in the background during the entire evening, but at one point in the evening, I gather everyone, give a mini-lecture on the composer, and invite everyone to be completely silent while we listen closely to some of the composer's best music.

I have no doubt that most of the members come for the wine and the fellowship, but they are also learning about the music. All of them are listening to music more now than when we started. Some are having their lives genuinely enriched through the experience.

DANCE

Jesus said, "We played the flute for you, / and you did not dance" (Matt. 11:17, NIV). Dance is a natural companion to music. Musical rhythms inspire movement. Just a few nights ago a close friend told me that her year-and-a-half-old granddaughter, with no prompting from any adult, began to dance, moving both arms and legs in rhythm the moment she heard music. Dance, like music, is part of our nature. When we do it, it allows us to express ourselves physically in a way that unites us with the music and with one another. When we see any type of dance performed by professionals—be it classical ballet, jazz, modern—we see the beauty and intricacy of the human body and the art it can make in motion.

My wife and I have the privilege every summer of attending performances of the American Dance Festival in Durham, North Carolina. The great dance companies of the world, including Pilobolus, Paul Taylor, and David Parsons, display a choreographical creativity that has us gawking in amazement year after year.

I wish that ballroom dancing would make a comeback. Although ballroom studios do not seem to lack for customers, places for ballroom dancing are much harder to find than they were twenty years ago. There is a real beauty and true romance in the waltzes, foxtrots, and tangos, and even people untrained in dance can participate.

For the ancient Hebrews, dance was a regular part of worship. In Psalm 150 we read, "Praise him with tambourine and dance" (v. 4). How ironic that so many of the conservative churches in America disdain dance—or prohibit it outright. When I was growing up near Wake Forest University, which was then controlled by the Southern Baptist Church, all forms of dancing were forbidden on campus. Dance was considered to be the work of the devil. Students protested, and the university eventually lifted the prohibition on dancing and even developed an excellent dance department. It also severed its affiliation with the Southern Baptist Church.

Liturgical dance has seen a renaissance in recent years. More and more liturgical dance companies are operating, and worship services increasingly include dance. Dance, like music, is a beautiful way to convey our worship of God.

Jesus invites us to the dance of life, both literally and metaphorically. The angels of heaven are often portrayed playing music on their trumpets and harps. Surely they, too, know the joy of the dance. Jesus calls us here on earth to sing the music and join in the dance of life.

Sydney Carter's hymn "Lord of the Dance" has become a favorite in many churches lately. Based on the melody of the old Shaker hymn "Simple Gifts" (which Aaron Copland used as a base tune for his ballet *Appalachian Spring*), "Lord of the Dance" offers image after image of a dancing Jesus and a dancing God. The words merit full quotation, and bring these thoughts on Jesus and the pleasure of music and dance to a fitting finale:

I danced in the morning
When the world was begun,
And I danced in the moon
And the stars and the sun,
And I came down from heaven
And I danced on the earth,
At Bethlehem
I had my birth.

Dance, then, wherever you may be,
I am the Lord of the Dance, said he,
And I'll lead you all, wherever you may be,
And I'll lead you all in the dance, said he.

I danced for the scribe
And the Pharisee,
But they would not dance
And they wouldn't follow me.
I danced for the fishermen,
For James and John—
They came with me
And the dance went on.
Chorus

I danced on the Sabbath
And I cured the lame;
The holy people
Said it was a shame.

They whipped and they stripped
And they hung me on high,
And they left me there
On a Cross to die.
Chorus

I danced on a Friday
When the sky turned black—
It's hard to dance
With the devil on your back
They buried my body
And they thought I'd gone
But I am the dance,
And I still go on,
Chorus

They cut me down
And I leapt up high;
I am the life
That'll never, never die;
I'll live in you
If you'll live in me—
I am the Lord
Of the Dance, said he.
Chorus

Words: Sydney Carter

6 / JESUS AND HEALTH

Nothing stands in the way of pleasure like physical pain or mental anguish. From all that we know about Jesus, he seems to have enjoyed the pleasure of good health up until the horrible miseries he endured on the last day of his life. Though his own suffering was short-lived, he made it the hallmark of his mission to care for those who were suffering. The Gospels tell us more stories of Jesus healing the sick than of his doing anything else.

Jesus operated within the conceptual understandings of his own people in his own time. Had Jesus lived in our time, I believe he would have been a physician on the forefront of medicine, seeking through science to cure our most dreaded diseases. But he lived in a time far removed from ours. Disease was understood to be caused by things such as sin, inherited sin, demons, bad star alignments, fates, and furies. The people of his time would have laughed at our own quaint notion that most diseases are caused by microscopic bacteria, viruses, and cancers that we cannot even see. Jesus carried out his healing ministry accordingly: he healed the sick through the power of his spirit.

JESUS AND THE MAN BORN BLIND

Jesus flat-out denied what most people in his own time saw as the main cause of disease. This story is in the Gospel of John. One Sabbath day, when Jesus saw a blind man, his disciples asked him, "Rabbi, who sinned, this man or his parents, that he was born blind?" (John 9:2). The question assumes that disease or disability is caused by sin—but whose sin? The man was born without sight, and his infirmity predated his ability to commit sins, so did his blindness result from the sin of his parents?

It was a theologically loaded question. The disciples were asking far more than they probably realized. If Jesus were to answer that the man's blindness came from his parents' sin, Jesus would be saying not just that *disease* is inherited but that *sin* is inherited. He would be stating the foundation of a Christian doctrine—namely, original sin—that St. Augustine would develop more than three-and-a-half centuries later and which to this day is one of the basic doctrines of most Churches.

Jesus did not answer the question that way. Jesus answered, "Neither this man nor his parents sinned; he was born blind so that God's works might be revealed in him" (John 9:3). The answer completely undercuts the question. Jesus did not share the assumption that disease is punishment for sin. Jesus saw disease not as punishment but as a two-part opportunity. First, it was an opportunity for healing. Second, it was an opportunity for revealing the work of God. Jesus never encountered a disease that he did not think could be healed. Jesus never encountered a patient whom he did not consider worthy of healing.

Jesus then healed the blind man in a way that seems primitive to us today. Jesus spat in the dust, made mud with the saliva, rubbed it on the man's eyes, then told him to go and wash himself in the pool of Siloam. The man returned from the pool fully able to see.

It is utterly useless for us to speculate on how Jesus did it. Did he have a chemical in his saliva that, mixed with dirt, became a healing balm? Jesus performed a similar healing in Mark 8:22–26. In this healing, Jesus did not quite get it right the first time. He put saliva on the man's eyes and asked him whether he could see anything. The man said, "I can see people, but they look like trees, walking" (v. 24). Then Jesus laid his hands on the man's eyes a second time, and the man's vision was restored completely. Some will contend that Jesus, being perfect, could not have made a mistake in this healing, that he must have intended a two-stage healing process. It seems more likely that here, as elsewhere, Mark is showing the true humanity as well as the true divinity of Jesus. The truly human Jesus might not get it perfectly right the first time, but he does not quit. He does not try to cover up his mistake in order to appear perfect. He is not concerned with his own perfection but with the man's blindness. Jesus is not satisfied when the man's vision is only partially restored. He wants the healing to be complete, and he keeps working with the patient until the healing is complete.

As we know, both Matthew and Luke used Mark's Gospel as a source for their own. But both chose to leave out this story from Mark. It is one of only a few Markan stories that are not found in Matthew or Luke or both. Perhaps they rejected this story because they felt it gave the impression that Jesus was less than perfect. Mark has no problems with the humanity of Jesus. The point for Mark is not that Jesus could make a mistake, but that Jesus kept at it until he got it right; he would not accept a halfway healed man as healed. Jesus knew the pleasure of good health and wanted that pleasure for everyone.

Let us return to the story of the blind man in John, chapter 9. After his healing, neighbors asked him how it was that he was healed. He answered in a totally straightforward and noninterpretive manner, "The man called Jesus made mud, spread it on my eyes, and said to me, 'Go to Siloam and wash.' Then I went and washed and received my sight" (v. 11).

When the healing is brought to the attention of the Pharisees, they are disturbed because Jesus had performed this healing on the Sabbath. They said to the healed man, "We know that this man [Jesus] is a sinner" (v. 24), for Jesus had broken the Sabbath rules. Unwilling at first to enter their theological discussion about Jesus, the man answers, "I do not know whether he is a sinner. One thing I do know, that though I was blind, now I see" (v. 25). The Pharisees then make the man retell the whole story, and at this point he does offer some theological speculation about Jesus. He says that he believes Jesus to be a prophet and not a sinner. He says that God does not listen to sinners, but that God apparently did listen to Jesus; otherwise Jesus would not have been able to heal him." The Pharisees dismiss the man as not knowing what he is talking about: "You were born entirely in sins, and are you trying to teach us?" (v. 34). The healed man will again encounter Jesus and worship him, and Jesus will again encounter the Pharisees, who will again fail to understand him.

Jesus cannot dissuade the Pharisees from their belief that disease is the result of sin. Jesus sees sin and disease as having nothing to do with each other. It is tragically ironic to hear some modern-day Christians claim that the AIDS epidemic is the result of sin, that sin being homosexuality. Judging from Jesus' clear message severing any connection between sin and disease, he could not have harbored so harsh a thought.

HEALING YOUR ENEMY

The story of the healing of a Roman centurion's slave is told in Matthew 8:5–13 and Luke 7:1–10, with some slight differences in details. The gist of the story is that the centurion comes to Jesus (in Luke, the centurion sends his message to Jesus via a group of Jewish elders). The centurion's slave is at home paralyzed, very sick, and close to death. We might surmise that the slave has had a stroke. Jesus offers to come to the house to heal him. The centurion (directly or through his messengers) tells Jesus that he does not need to come to the house, that he does not consider himself worthy of having Jesus come into his house. Jesus says of the centurion, "Not even in Israel have I found such faith" (Luke 7:9). Jesus heals the slave at a distance that very hour.

The term *centurion* literally means "commander of one hundred," but centurions were often commanders of much larger numbers of Roman soldiers. Roman centurions were hated by the Jews of Palestine. They were soldiers of an occupying army who did not believe in the God of the Jews and who treated the Jews with disdain and often brutality. (In Luke's version of the story, this particular centurion, unlike most, has treated Jews favorably in the past.) The Jews considered the Romans to be unclean according to the laws of God, and that to have anything to do with them was to make oneself unclean. The typical reaction of pious Jews such as the Pharisees was to act as if the Romans were not there and did not exist. They would not even look at Romans, much less speak to them or do anything else that could be regarded as being friendly with them.

Perhaps the centurion is even a believer in the Jewish God, one of the so-called God-fearers, gentiles who believed in the Jewish God but did not go so far as to undergo circumcision and become actual Jews.

That Jesus healed the Roman centurion's slave raises many questions for us, just as it must have for the earliest Christians. The first question has to do with the existence of slavery in Jesus' time. Matthew and Luke use different words to describe the slave. Matthew uses the Greek word *pais,* which is translated in the NRSV as "servant." Luke uses the Greek word *doulos,* translated as "slave." Although the words are different, the variation between *pais* and *doulos,* servant and slave, is slight. The young man who needed healing was doubtless a servant to the centurion, but he was not a *free* servant. He did not have the power to change his circumstances. All servants in the Roman army were, in this sense, slaves.

We might question, then, why Jesus did not tell the centurion to set his slave free. In fact, we have no record of Jesus ever speaking against the institution of slavery. Jesus, like virtually everyone else in the first-century Roman world, accepted slavery as a normal social arrangement. Slavery in Jesus' time was quite different from slavery in the Americas in the seventeenth through the nineteenth centuries. It was not based on race; anyone could be a slave, and anyone could be free. Slaves could work for and buy their freedom, and a whole class in Roman society, called freedmen, comprised ex-slaves and their children. Slaves in Roman society were not thought of as inferior beings; they were merely thought to be less fortunate. However much we might wish that Jesus had expressed antislavery sentiments, he seems to have accepted it as a societal norm.

The second question the story raises involves the relationship between Jesus and the gentiles. Although Jesus did not himself feel bound to follow all the Jewish laws in the Torah in regard to ritual purity and Sabbath observance, he did keep his mission almost entirely among his own people. He chose no gentiles as his disciples, nor were there any gentiles among the women who followed him. He told his disciples, "Go nowhere among the Gentiles, and enter no towns of the Samaritans, but go rather to the lost sheep of the house of Israel" (Matt. 10:5–6). Jesus never ventured far from Jewish territory and rarely had dealings with gentiles. Although Jesus heals the centurion's slave, he never comes into direct contact with the slave or even sees him. In Luke's version of the story, Jesus never comes into contact with the centurion either. Despite customary Jewish behavior and Jesus' own focus on his mission to the Jews, Jesus showed his love for these gentiles, even while keeping his contact with them to a minimum. The time for the mission to the gentiles had not yet come.

The story raises a third question, one that the Church might rather avoid, about the relationship between the centurion and his slave. Among the many practices in the Roman army that the Jews regarded as unclean before God was the practice of homosexuality, which frequently occurred between older Roman military officers and younger male slaves. Such relationships, like virtually all relationships in Roman society, were hierarchical. Homosexual relationships among Roman soldiers were always relationships between an officer and a slave, never relationships among equals. Could this have been the relationship between the centurion and his "slave-boy," as the word *pais* in Luke could possibly be translated? Such a relationship would explain the Roman centurion's obvious deep concern and love for his slave, and provide motivation for the centurion's desperate choice to go to a Jewish faith healer for help.

These issues—slavery, Roman-Jewish relations, sexuality—do not seem to matter to Jesus. What matters is that the slave is near death and the centurion's faith is strong—as Jesus says, "I tell you, not even in Israel have I found such faith" (Luke 7:9). Jesus can and does restore the slave to health. Jesus consistently seeks a better quality of life not only for those who are considered good and morally upright or for members of his own ethnic and religious group, but for everyone.

JESUS AND WOMEN'S HEALTH

Women's health was of little concern in the world of late Mediterranean antiquity. In our own time and culture, women outlive men by an average of eight years. In Jesus' time it was quite the reverse. In the age before birth control, the rigors of nearly constant pregnancy and childbearing took a serious toll on women's lives. Grandmothers, who play such a significant role in our own society, are rarely mentioned in the Bible, for women seldom reached the age of grandmotherhood.

The primary women's health issue in Jesus' time was that of satisfactory pregnancy and childbirth. The medical profession, to the extent that it existed, was entirely male, and limited its resources and treatments largely to men. These male doctors, knowing very little about women's diseases, did the best they could, but spent most of their time on male patients. The society had a higher expectation than we do that women should suffer in silence. A subspecialty of the medical profession, midwifery, was given over to women. Beyond this, women's treatment was limited largely to mothers caring for daughters and for their own mothers.

In our chapter on Jesus and women, we saw that Jesus included women in all aspects of his ministry. Although Jesus' healing powers did not change the entire course of public health during his lifetime, Jesus did show a concern for women's health, both physical and mental, that was unknown during this time.

The story of the woman with the twelve-year menstrual problem (Mark 5:25–34) is a brief but effective example. We have already gone over this story in detail, so we need only note a few things about it here. The difficulty of this woman's gynecological problems must have been extreme as well as chronic. She had not only sought medical attention, but over the years "she had endured much under many physicians, and had spent all that she had; and she was no better, but rather grew worse" (v. 26). She came to Jesus, grappling through the crowd, only to be able to touch the hem of his garment. Her condition had made her desperate, but her faith was strong, and she could feel the healing happening inside her body from the moment she touched his garment. Even though he did not see her, Jesus also knew that something had happened, that power had flowed out from him. When he looked around, the woman came before him and "in fear and trembling, fell down before him, and told him the whole truth" (v. 33). Jesus' response is, "Daughter, your faith has made you well; go in peace, and be healed of your disease" (v. 34).

Though this healing diverted time from what seemed to be the more pressing task of healing the daughter of Jairus, who was near death, Jesus took the time to talk with the woman. Jesus was concerned not only with matters of life and death but also with chronic illness, with the sort of debilitating pain that may not threaten life but greatly diminishes its quality. Jesus wanted this woman to be able to enjoy the goodness that life had for her. That she was a woman, that she was suffering from gynecological problems that made her ritually unclean, and that she was a nameless nobody did not matter to him. She showed faith in him and never gave up hope of getting better. This meant something to Jesus, and provided the opportunity to demonstrate that the pleasures of good health should be available to all of us.

JESUS AND MENTAL HEALTH

Jesus lived at a time when most of the things we would call mental illness were generally, though not universally, understood to be caused by demon possession. Jesus chose to deal with mental health problems within the context that most first-century people understood. The basic difference between their understanding and ours is that they thought mental illness came from forces outside a person; we think of mental illness as problems within a person. It is becoming increasingly apparent, through medical research, that many mental health issues are chemically based and are not problems or flaws in the character of a person. Jesus understood this, on some level, long before we did.

Translations of the Bible sometimes blur the distinction between the ancient and the modern understandings of mental illness. For example, in one story a man is described, in the original Greek text, as *selniazesthe.* The Greek word literally means that he was "moonstruck." English translations almost always render this Greek word as "epileptic," giving the impression that the original writers and readers understood the man's symptoms in the same way we do today. The ancients knew the *symptoms* of what we call epilepsy, but they believed the causes had something to do with the positioning and effects of the moon. We do not share that first-century conceptual framework, nor should we. Like Jesus, we need to be about the process of healing the illness. We do not understand or treat the illness the same way, but we do seek the same result—healing.

In recent years we have made tremendous strides in the treatment of various mental illnesses. In the early and mid-twentieth century, we thought that most mental illness would eventually be cured by psychoanalysis. Now we are finding that more mental illnesses can be treated by drug therapies. People who suffer from debilitating and suicidal depression are more and more able to lead good and fruitful lives because of drug therapies. Even the most severe form of mental illness, schizophrenia, is responding to new drug therapies. The research scientists who create these drugs, the physicians who test and administer these drugs, and the pharmacologists who dispense them are no less healers than was Jesus. We heal in a different manner, but with the same purpose—to improve the quality and fullness of life.

Another factor involved in the healing process is society's response to the sick. Many of the sick were shunned by their families and their communities during Jesus' time. If they were considered unclean, they were barred from public worship. If they were thought to be possessed by demons, they were scrupulously avoided. These were the very people who most frequently sought Jesus for help. He never turned them down. He never shied away from them. He undoubtedly cared about those who were both physically and mentally ill and thereby marginalized by their own communities.

JESUS' MISSION AND OURS

Some of us are involved in the health-care professions. All of us are involved in health care. Our ways of practicing health care are for the most part different than those of Jesus'. In some ways, however, our practices would be improved if they were more similar to those of Jesus'.

We do not tend to think of Jesus in the same category as a medical doctor. We tend to see him as a spiritual teacher and healer. If we compare Jesus to modern individuals, it is more likely that so-called faith healers come to mind. At the same time, few in the medical profession look to Jesus as a model. What little attention they may pay to medicine in antiquity is seen in the Hippocratic oath or in some vague awareness of ancient physicians like Galen or when employing the medicinal properties of certain herbs that were discovered by ancient cultures such as the Chinese. Not many courses in medical schools on the history of medicine go back any further than the early modern period.

On the other hand, many proponents of "alternative medicine" tend to avoid standard medical treatment whenever possible, in favor of unconventional approaches that are less invasive, are less reliant on drugs, and use a variety of techniques like herbal treatments, chiropractic, and acupuncture. But Jesus does not typically figure into this health-care model any more than the conventional one.

Do the healing stories in the Gospels have any relevance for our understanding of healing today? Or are they simply stories that show the power of God and the goodness of Jesus in an ancient time? I would suggest that in a number of ways we can and do see Jesus as a medical model.

First, Jesus treated every sick person he came in contact with regardless of that person's station in life or past history. He showed no prejudice toward people who were not of his own ethnic or religious group. He even treated people who were the enemies of his own people. He treated as many females as he did males—something remarkable in his male-dominated culture—and treated them all equally. Jesus saw equal value in every life. He even, indeed often, treated lepers, the outcasts of society, whom no one else would go near. He treated people without regard to age; from small children to the old and infirm, Jesus never turned down a single person who came to him for treatment.

For the most part, we adhere today to Jesus' principle of equality in dispensing treatment, but we still have far too many instances of people who are effectively denied treatment because they lack health insurance. If Jesus is our model, we need to create a situation in which every person in the United States has adequate access to health care. Although in many respects the United States has the best medical treatment in the world, when it comes to providing quality health care to poor people, we fall short. Insurance policies are couched in legal language that is readable only by those who are trained to read insurance policies. People often have to pay excessive amounts of money for treatments that they thought were covered by their insurance. No one would buy something as expensive as a car without knowing the price they were going to have to pay for it. Yet people will undergo a wide variety of medical procedures without the faintest idea of how much it is going to cost. Doctors tend not to know the patient costs for the procedures they perform. If you ask for an estimate of charges after insurance before you go into a hospital, you are not likely to get an answer. People then get stuck with huge medical bills that consume life savings and future incomes.

I had a radically different experience of hospital treatment when I was in England in 1995. I was among the leaders of a study tour of eighty students. I got an infection in my foot that swelled so badly that I could not put my shoe on, and within a couple of days, I could not walk at all. Another faculty member took me to the nearest hospital, St. Mary's (where, incidentally, penicillin had been discovered back in 1937). I went into a waiting room they called "Casualty," which we would call the emergency room. The attendant took my name, and that was all. She did not ask for insurance information or even what country I was from. She just told me to sit on a bench across from her and a nurse would come. The nurse took several other people, all of whom appeared to be in worse shape than I was, before she took me. In about twenty minutes I was taken to an examination room, where a doctor and nurse diagnosed a cellulitis infection, prescribed medicine for me, gave me a "tubi-grip" (something like an Ace bandage that is cut off in rolls), and directed me to the hospital pharmacy. The pharmacist asked, "Do you pay for your prescriptions?" Not being a British citizen, I assumed that I did. He gave me my two prescriptions. My cost was five pounds, about eight dollars. The whole process took less than an hour. No questions were asked of me other than my name and the doctor's various diagnostic questions about the condition of my foot. The prescriptions worked, and within a few days my foot was back to normal.

I certainly cannot vouch for British medicine always working so well. The British frequently complain about their national health service. But I can say that patient care, regardless of who the patient is and how much the patient or the patient's insurance can pay, was the primary concern of the doctors and administrators. In this way the dispensation of medical treatment had more in common with Jesus' way of healing than I had ever experienced.

Second, Jesus never considered any disease or medical condition to be incurable. He took on all cases. Moreover, his goal was not just to diminish pain and make life bearable but to cure people and restore them to complete good health. The Gospel stories tell of his being able to do that instantaneously. It is not so easy or quick for us, but the goal ought to be the same, both in terms of treatment of individual patients now and research for future cures for diseases.

I just talked to my brother on the telephone. Had he lived before 1923, he would have died at a young age because he is diabetic. The discovery of insulin made possible a high quality of life for millions of people who previously had no hope. Jesus' principle is that no disease exists for which there is not a cure. We need to devote greater resources, both human and financial, to the quest for the cure and prevention of AIDS, cancers, and various other diseases that still cause so much pain and death in our time.

Although we all must die at some time, there is no good reason why so many of us must suffer so much during the years that we have. We should not only seek to cure and prevent diseases, we should also seek ways to decrease and eliminate pain. Many people suffer from diseases or conditions that are not life threatening but bring so much pain that they dramatically lower the quality of life. Jesus sought to end the pain and suffering of those who came to him. The goodness and pleasures of life are radically diminished by chronic pain.

When Jesus healed someone, he never went halfway. He thought of a human being as a unity of body and spirit. This understanding is embedded in the Hebrew word *nefesh,* a concept Jesus understood well. Our *nefesh* is all that we are as persons. It is our mind, our soul, our body, our spirit, our very being. When any part of it is not functioning properly, the whole is out of balance. This is why Jesus sought to heal not only physical infirmities but mental conditions as well. In the story of Jesus healing the paralytic (Mark 2:1–12), Jesus does not merely heal the body, he forgives the sins. The Pharisees do not dispute his authority to heal the sick, but they do say, "Why does this fellow speak in this way? It is blasphemy! Who can forgive sins but God alone?" (v. 7). Though it was made clear in the story of Jesus healing the blind man, in John, chapter 9, that Jesus did not believe that sin was the cause of illness, he did understand that no one is a whole being if only the body is whole. A spirit free from the burdens of anxiety and sin is essential for human wholeness.

The third lesson we can learn from Jesus is that healing goes both ways. It was not just the healer who brought the healing; it was also the faith of the person who was healed. Sometimes when he healed a person, Jesus would say, "Go in peace; your faith has made you well." On one occasion he found that when faith was lacking, healing was limited. In his own hometown of Nazareth, he received less respect for his mission than he had anywhere else. Mark says, "And they took offense at him. Then Jesus said to them, 'Prophets are not without honor, except in their hometown, and among their own kin, and in their own house.' And he could do no deed of power there, except that he laid his hands on a few sick people and cured them. And he was amazed at their unbelief" (6:3–6).

It is not our purpose here to debate the age-old theological questions about the relationships between Jesus and God and between God and humanity. But it is clear that Jesus did not consider himself to be working alone. He needed the faith of those whom he healed, or their loved ones; he needed the help of the apostles and many other friends; he also needed the help of God.

One of the clearest messages that Jesus brings to us, yet one we still have so much difficulty understanding, is that God is our coworker. Our old understanding of God as sitting high in God's heaven, remote and removed from the affairs of humankind, touching humanity with healing grace at one point and deadly plagues at another, is not the understanding of God with which Jesus worked.

THE PLEASURES OF SCIENCE AND LEARNING

The image of a remote and static God has often led us astray from the character and purpose of the mission Jesus left us. It has led some Christians to believe and teach that religion is opposed to science. In the sixteenth century, Galileo and Copernicus brought down the wrath of the Church on themselves because they believed that the world was round and was not the center of the universe. It would take the Church a long time to catch up with science on this one. Now the heretic Galileo is honored by the Church and buried in one of the holy churches of Catholicism, Santa Croce, in Florence, Italy.

Nowadays many Christians consider Darwin and the theory of evolution to be great enemies of the faith. The reality, I believe, is quite the opposite. God created the universe. God created the processes by which the universe works. God left it to humanity to discover these processes and use them for the world's benefit. One of these processes is biological evolution. God is not against evolution; God created it. Millions of pieces of evidence in the fossil and DNA records show conclusively that species evolve from other species. Even Pope John Paul II, in 1993, accepted on behalf of the Roman Catholic Church that evolution was the process by which God formed and forms life in the universe. Yes, humanlike species did precede us: *Australopithecus,* Homo habilis, and Homo erectus; we have bones of all of them. At some point our species, Homo sapiens, evolved on the dusty plains of Africa, not from monkeys but from other hominid species that preceded us. Eventually a man and a woman came about through evolution who possessed all the characteristics that identify us as a species. All human DNA can be traced back to these, our common ancestors.

The genius of the authors of Genesis is their understanding that the earliest humans were the first creatures to relate to God. The authors of Genesis had no intention of writing a literal history of humanity. Rather, they wrote a beautiful and compelling story of God's creation and humanity's role in it. They even used symbolic names for the first man and woman. The Hebrew word *adham,* which we bring into English as *Adam,* means "humankind." The Hebrew we bring into English as *Eve* means "living being."

Our current understanding of what is sometimes called "theistic evolution" shows the glory of God in creating such a magnificently complex universe. The great twentieth-century French paleontologist and Catholic priest, Pierre Teilhard de Chardin, was perhaps the first to realize the theological implications of evolution. In his many books, he discerned the handiwork of God in the complexity of evolutionary creation.

Another scientific theory likewise demonstrates the genius of the authors of Genesis. That theory, known colloquially as the "big bang theory," derives from many years of astronomers' observations that all the galaxies of the universe are moving away from one another at a rapid but steady speed. Because they all are steadily moving away from one another at the same speed indicates that they all must have been together in one massive ball of matter at the beginning of time. The first words of God in the Bible are, accordingly, "Let there be light" (Gen. 1:3). Light results from any explosion of mass. All light ultimately resulted from this great explosion of mass that was God's creation of the universe.

Science, like everything else, lies within the realm of God. God is the ultimate creator of all science. Part of the human condition, and a crown of human glory, is the need to discern these principles of nature and to learn how to make life and the world around us better through that discernment. Primitive humans discerned that fire, which held such potential danger and destruction, could be tamed and used to increase the quality of human life. Today we still have so much to learn. Pitting religion against science serves no human or divine purpose, and ultimately prevents us from sharing in the abundant life to which Jesus called us all.

JESUS AND OUR HEALTH

Jesus serves in many ways as an example for us in the art and science of health care. He treated all people's health concerns equally, he never gave up on a case, he gave equal importance to mental and physical health, and he sought the complete and full recovery of the people he helped. Above all, he points us to the knowledge that healing is not just physical or emotional—it is also spiritual.

If we believe that Jesus is something more than a historical figure, and if we believe that Jesus is in some way a living presence today, then it is fitting for us to include him and what he taught in our healing efforts today. Many medical studies have been conducted over the last several years of the effects of prayer on the healing process. Too many of these studies have not had proper controls or have been analyzed by people who were biased about the outcomes, and therefore have yielded unreliable results. Yet it is clear that none of these studies, at least to my knowledge, has ever shown that faith or prayer has a negative effect on the healing process.

When a person has a meaningful life, has other people who love and care for him or her, and has a positive outlook on the value of his or her own life, that person has a better chance of healing. Perhaps the most positive person I have ever encountered is my own mother. I have sometimes thought of her as a "Pollyanna," someone who always believes that things will get better and who never quite faces the bad things of life. A year ago, after suffering terribly for more than a year with intestinal ailments that doctors failed to accurately diagnose, my father took her to the emergency room. She was in great pain, and clearly on the verge of death. The examination found that a large, cancerous tumor, previously undiagnosed, was causing intestinal blockage. The tumor was successfully removed, but afterward my wife and I could do nothing but comfort my dad; at that point it appeared that her chance for survival was quite small. The surgeon, however, had encouraging words, and during the course of the next month in the hospital, my mother, with her faith and her strong positive attitude, lived up to that encouragement. She spent her time not just on her own recovery but also caring for the overworked nurses who were caring for her. Within two weeks she knew the name and life story of every patient, nurse, and orderly on her floor. Her spirit inspired them and, I am sure, contributed to her own healing.

After a month, she was released from the hospital. Scarcely any of the people who saw her go into the hospital expected to see her come out alive. Two months later, she and my father danced at my son's wedding. Now, a year later, she and my father are about to move into a new house, an eventuality none of us would have dreamed of just a year ago.

Can we detect the hand of God in all of this? The architect Mies van der Rohe first said, "God is in the details." Certainly my mother received the prayers of many when she was in such terrible condition and horrible pain. Her full and remarkably quick recovery, though unusual, could not be classified as a miracle. If we think of a miracle as God's direct intervention in the affairs of humans, my mother's recovery would not qualify. No healer like Jesus said to her, "Be healed, arise, and return to your home." It was rather a team of two surgeons, a father and daughter, who cut the sickness out of her body and restitched and stapled it to the point that she would be able to recover. Yet I had the feeling through it all that God was in the details, that God's healing presence filled that hospital and helped restore my mother's health and pleasure in life. Pain diminishes pleasure. Jesus knew this and did all he could to care for people who were in pain, to bring healing to them. We are not equipped to make scientific historical judgments on every miraculous healing attributed to Jesus in the Bible. But the abundance of healing stories and the consistency with which they appear throughout the Gospels is clear evidence that Jesus considered healing to be a major part of his ministry.

Jesus did not have the advantages of modern medicine and medical training. He worked within the realm of what was possible in first-century Palestine. We have come a long way since the time of Jesus, and he has come with us. We still have a long way to go. If Jesus goes with us, the journey will be better for his presence. He is still a healer.

7 / JESUS AND LOVE

There is an old cliché, "The Greeks had a word for it." A cliché is a saying that has been so often repeated that it loses the full force of its meaning. As a fifty-seven-year-old university professor, I sometimes feel like I preside over the generation gap. Phrases that had become clichés in my generation are not known to the students I teach. If I were to use a phrase like "lock, stock, and barrel," most of my students would have only a vague idea of what I was talking about. My students, of course, have their own clichés, derived from their own culture, that their parents would not recognize.

This difference also passes over to their knowledge of famous people. When I ask my students who Albert Schweitzer was, few have ever heard of him. To my generation, this Nobel Prize–winning missionary, medical doctor, musicologist, and biblical scholar was not only the most famous Christian but perhaps the most famous person of the era. In contrast, all my students have heard of and can tell you something about Mother Teresa or Nelson Mandela.

"The Greeks had a word for it" was a cliché already passing from usage during my generation's coming of age. Yet it is a rich saying, full of meaning for anyone who studies the Greek language, the language in which the New Testament was written. Greek is a language of much greater subtlety and expressiveness than English. It often displays clearer lines of meaning than does English because it has a much larger basic vocabulary than English and is more grammatically complex.

When I am teaching Greek, I try not to tell my students how complex any particular aspect of the language is, compared to English, until they have learned it. For example, English has two forms of the participle, the present active (*-ing* words like *running, jumping, learning*) and the past passive (*-ed* words like *loved, rolled, boosted*). English, which has no present passive participle or past active participle, is a defective language when it comes to participles. Greek, however, has 192 forms of the participle, and the Greeks use them constantly. Protecting my students from this fact as they learn the participles seems to make the going a little less tough on them.

Greek vocabulary can also be daunting. Greek has far more basic vocabulary words than English, though English has more total words because of its immense amount of technical vocabulary. Often it takes several words in English to say what one Greek word will say. I remember a friend of mine who was struggling in second-year Greek class. He nearly reached the end of his rope (another cliché, but one that most of my students would know) one day while translating in class. He came to a word he could not remember or did not know. The professor chastised him for not knowing that this word meant "to hit a running boar with a spear." That is eight words in English to say what one word meant in Greek.

THE WORDS OF LOVE

English vocabulary is inadequate when it comes to the word *love.* This single word in English has so many meanings that people can get into trouble over the use of it. A person can say it with one meaning, while the person to whom it is said hears another meaning. We easily understand the difference between the statements, "I love Marianne" and "I love tomatoes." We less easily understand the difference between the phrases "I love Marianne" (my wife) and "I love Becky" (a friend of ours for many years). If I say, "I love Becky," Marianne, Becky, and Becky's husband, Nelson, all know what I mean. Others might not. We need to be careful about the way we use the word *love.*

In Greek, especially ancient Greek, it is much less of a problem. The Greeks have several words for *love,* each of which refers to a different type of love. Each word makes distinctions that our single English word does not. C. S. Lewis, the great Renaissance literature scholar who became far better known as a lay Christian writer, wrote a book called *The Four Loves,* in which he described four different Greek words that speak of four different types of love. Lewis highlighted that particularly Christian Greek word for love, *agape.* Lewis's basic ideas on these words are well known.

The Greek word *storge* means love in the familial context, in particular the love of a parent for a child. Certainly this kind of love deserves its own word, for it is something far different from the other kinds of human love. Nonetheless, it was used sparingly in ancient Greek, and not at all in the New Testament.

A second Greek word for love is *eros.* It was the word commonly used in the classical period, before the beginnings of Christianity. Our English word *erotic* derives from it. It conveys the meaning of romantic love, love between a man and a woman, but is also used in classical Greek for various other types of love. For reasons that are not completely clear, but probably have to do with the frequent sexual connotations of the word, early Christians tended to avoid its use.

The third Greek word is *philia.* This word conveys the love experienced in close friendship. We derive an enormous number of English words from *philia.* Put it together with the Greek word *adelphos,* which means "brother," and we get *Philadelphia,* the "city of brotherly love." The use of the words *eros* and *philia* can help avoid the misunderstandings that the single English word *love* can sometimes produce. I have *eros* for Marianne; I have *philia* for Becky. No problem.

We also get a lot of our *-phile* words in English from *philia.* An Anglophile is someone who loves England and things English. An audiophile is someone who loves good sound and good sound-producing equipment. Perhaps the strangest of such words in English is hemophilia, the prefix *hemo* coming from the Greek word for blood. The word for this terrible disease in which blood does not clot and a person keeps on bleeding, means, etymologically, "love of blood."

Because Christians were uncomfortable with the word *eros,* they soon took up a new Greek word for love, *agape,* and used it as their own special word with their own special meaning. The early Christians did not invent the word. It had already been used by the Jewish rabbis who translated the Hebrew Scriptures into Greek. But the early Christians, consciously or unconsciously, did seek to give the word a certain newness of meaning. It became the word to express God's love for humanity, divine love. It was the love God showed us in Jesus Christ, the love that Jesus himself so frequently showed for others, and the kind of love that we, through Christ, can have for one another, and even for our enemies.

AGAPE IN THE LETTERS OF PAUL AND JOHN

"Love Is Patient . . ."

Two great chapters in the New Testament deal with the idea of love as *agape.* In the thirteenth chapter of Paul's First Letter to the Corinthians, the apostle comes as close as anyone to defining the meaning of *agape,* the word that he uses throughout the chapter. Paul writes:

> Love is patient; love is kind; love is not envious or boastful or arrogant or rude. It does not insist on its own way; it is not irritable or resentful; it does not rejoice in wrongdoing, but rejoices in the truth. It bears all things, believes all things, hopes all things, endures all things.
>
> Love never ends. . . . And now faith, hope, and love abide, these three; and the greatest of these is love (vv. 4–8, 13).

It is with good reason that this chapter is almost always read at Christian weddings. If a wife and husband will maintain for each other all the characteristics of love described here, their marriage will be blessed and happy.

From time to time, people have suggested to me that because 1 Corinthians, chapter 13, is about divine love, *agape,* and not romantic love, *eros,* it is actually not appropriate for Christian weddings. Such thinking misses the point. The early Christians avoided the word *eros.* They meant for their new word, *agape,* to convey the idea that the quality of love that God has for humanity is the quality of love that a woman and a man can have for each other. When the author of the Letter to the Ephesians (traditionally considered to be Paul, but that is not certain) says, "Husbands should love their wives as they do their own bodies" (5:28), he, like Paul, uses the word *agape.* For these early Christian writers, sexual, romantic love could have the same quality as divine love.

"God Is Love"

The second great New Testament chapter on love, though not as well known as 1 Corinthians, chapter 13, is perhaps even more profound. It is the fourth chapter of the First Letter of John. This may be the most important chapter in the entire Bible. Here the New Testament defines God and God's relationship with humanity in terms of *agape* love. The passage concisely touches on every major theme of the New Testament and deals with each theme in what seems to me is the proper proportion. It begins:

> Beloved, let us love one another, because love is from God; everyone who loves is born of God and knows God. Whoever does not love does not know God, for God is love (vv.7–8).

The first thing we might notice about this profound and almost shocking statement is that it does not equate being "from God" or "of God" with believing any particular thing about God or about Jesus Christ. The statement does not limit God's love to Christians. *Anyone* who has love is born of God, regardless of that person's religious beliefs. The corollary is almost as shocking. "Whoever does not love does not know God" implies that many who consider themselves "of God" by virtue of having made a Christian confession fall short. The Orthodox Christian Serbs, for example, who massacred hundreds of Muslims in Kosovo, would not seem to demonstrate the *agape* that is a characteristic of being born "of God." The same could be said of the racists, anti-Semites, misogynists, and homophobes in our own country who define themselves in terms of hatred while at the same time confessing Christian beliefs at church on Sunday.

The words that conclude the eighth verse of the chapter, and which are repeated in verse sixteen, are the most important words in the Bible: "God is *agape*." Although "God is love" is a statement so commonly heard that it may be a cliché, it is well worth thinking fully about the implications of the statement. The author of the letter goes so far in his understanding of love as to define *God* as love. He pointedly does not define God in terms of power but in terms of what is in some ways the opposite of power.

In his First Letter to the Corinthians, Paul remarks that "God's weakness is stronger than human strength" (1:25). This is not just hyperbole; Paul is not saying that God is so strong that even those things about God that might be weak are still stronger than anything we humans might possess. No, Paul is *really* talking about the weakness of God. Paul understands this weakness as having been perfectly expressed in Christ's life on earth and his death on the cross. The messiah did not come as a great king. He was not Augustus Caesar. He was not, to use Käsemann's phrase once more, "God astride the earth." He came as a humble worker who spoke a message of love, even love for his enemies and the enemies of his people. His humiliating death reflected the weakness of God, but also expressed a profound but difficult way to comprehend the love of God.

John's letter continues:

> God's love was revealed among us in this way: God sent his only Son into the world so that we might live through him. In this is love, not that we love God but that he loved us and sent his son to be the atoning sacrifice for our sins (4:9–10).

Here the author of the letter puts his major theological points in good order. God's love is the first point. Christ's life in the world is the second. Our ability to live lives of love through Christ is the third. Christ as the atoning sacrifice for our sins is the last.

Too often Christians get the last point but miss the first three. Too many think of God as having sent Jesus for the sole purpose of dying as a human sacrifice for the sins of the rest of us. Though John does not deny the reality of the atonement, he does not go into any lengthy theological effort to explain it, as Paul does in Romans. John does not see the atonement as the most important thing in the Christian faith. Jesus did not come to die on the cross. Jesus came "into the world so that we might live through him." The Christian faith is not about death; it is about life. As Jesus said, in a passage we have already looked at, "I came that they may have life, and have it abundantly" (John 10:10).

Living through Jesus

Although we cannot be sure that the author of the First Letter of John is the same person who wrote the fourth Gospel, or that he had ever read any of the other Gospels, he does perhaps more than any other writer in the New Testament have a true grasp of the message of Jesus. He knows to the depths of his being what it is to live through Jesus. We can know this, too.

We should probably first understand, however, that living through Jesus is not the same thing as living like Jesus. Few of us are called to be itinerant preachers, faith healers, or demon exorcists. None of us wears robes and sandals to work every day. All of us, however much we may complain about it, are immersed in twenty-first-century American culture. We operate within our culture and its thought framework, just as Jesus operated within his. What, then, does it mean to live through Jesus in the twenty-first century? The First Letter of John continues:

> Beloved, since God loved us so much, we also ought to love one another. No one has ever seen God; if we love one another, God lives in us, and his love is perfected in us.
>
> By this we know that we abide in him and he in us, because he has given us of his Spirit. . . .
>
> God is love, and those who abide in love abide in God, and God abides in them. Love has been perfected among us in this (4:11–13, 16–17).

If we think about it, the theology of this statement is so powerful as to overwhelm us. God is described here not as omnipotent or omniscient, a grand and glorious father in the heavens sitting on his majestic throne waiting to wreak the vengeance of judgment on us (or at least on all but a few of us) at the end of the world. Neither is God a mysterious "force" in the universe whose ways are discernible only to the enlightened. God is not a best buddy or a functional imaginary friend who walks with me and talks with me.

God is love.

Few of us came to know God directly through an experience in which God appeared to us or spoke to us from a burning bush or a whirlwind. We came to know God because some other human being told us about God. For most of us, that person was a parent. That parent said a blessing with us at the table or prayers with us when we went to bed at night. That parent took us to Sunday school or church, where we learned more about God. That parent also loved us, and in so doing, showed us what God was all about. For most of us, our childhood understanding of God stems from the way we understood our parents. God loves us and cares for us in a way that is similar to but greater than that of our parents. Those of us who had parents who did not show us God's love, who were abusive or violent, had God imaged to us in other ways. We thought of God as either judgmental, abusive, and violent like our parent, or as the antithesis of our parent, as the loving parent figure we wanted to have. In either case, no one is more crucial in communicating an understanding of God to a child than the child's parent. And the one thing we learn about God through a parent's care for us is God's love.

That most basic understanding of God tends to dissipate for many of us as we get older. Some of us tend to forget about God, often times if not altogether.

Others of us may be turned toward the harsher, more judgmental understandings of God that are taught by many churches and denominations.

As his disciples shooed a group of children away from him, Jesus said to them, "Let the little children come to me; do not stop them; for it is to such as these that the kingdom of God belongs" (Mark 10:14). The child's understanding of God is relational. The child knows God's love in the parent's love. That love is what we know of God.

A story told in a sermon by Rev. Susan Jones, a United Methodist minister from Duke University Divinity School, illustrates my point about learning God's love through our parent's love better than any other illustration I have.

Susan tells of her young son Ben. Having been brought up in a home with two United Methodist ministers as parents, Ben was familiar with church matters. He had been to Ash Wednesday services and seen the administration of ashes to penitents' foreheads in the form of a cross. He had been to baptismal renewal services and seen the water applied to persons' foreheads in the form of a cross.

When Ben was nine, Susan was putting him to bed one night. They said their prayers, she tucked him in, and she kissed him good night. As she started to rise, Ben said, "Wait, Mom." He took her head in both his hands, pulled her close, and gave her eight kisses on the forehead, five down and three across. He then said, "Mom, you are blessed." Susan was taken aback. It took her a moment to realize that the kisses on the forehead had made the shape of a cross. She said, "Ben, do you realize that you kissed me in the form of a cross?" "Yes, Mom," he replied, "I planned it that way."

All of us can return our mother's love, but in that moment of grace between Susan Jones and her son, I suspect she experienced God's love in a new and deeper way than ever before. When Paul wrote, "Love never ends" (1 Cor. 13:8), he may have meant more than just the chronological persistence of love. Love never ceases expressing itself in new and fresh ways.

This may be an odd analogy, but perhaps it conveys a truth about love. As we learn more and more about viruses, cancers, and bacteria, we learn how resilient and adaptable they are. It is difficult to kill them off; they will learn new ways to live, new ways to thwart the agents of their destruction. Love is likewise constantly finding new ways to create and preserve its own existence, even in the most unloving of hosts.

JESUS ON LOVE

When we look through the Gospels, we find that Jesus had less to say about love than we would have expected. Unlike the Greek philosopher Plato, whose dialogue *Symposium* is entirely about love, Jesus spoke of love only a few times. Jesus would leave it to Paul and the author of the First Letter of John to define *agape* love. When Jesus did speak about love, he seldom used the noun. He more often used the verb form, as in this beautiful passage in Mark's Gospel. When a scribe asked him, "Which commandment is the first of all?" Jesus answered,

> "The first is, 'Hear, O Israel: the Lord our God, the Lord is one; you shall love the Lord your God with all your heart, and with all your soul, and with all your mind, and with all your strength.' The second is this, 'You shall love your neighbor as yourself.' There is no other commandment greater than these" (12:28–31).

Jesus' statement is both a preservation of an ancient Jewish statement, the prayer called the Shema, from Deuteronomy 6:4, and a new twist on that statement.

The prayer is called the Shema because its first word in Hebrew is *Shema,* which means "hear" or "hearken." Long before the time of Jesus, the Shema had already become the central prayer in Judaism. Even to this day, it occupies a position in Judaism that is roughly similar to the position of the Lord's Prayer in Christianity. Jesus grew up saying it in the synagogue and in his own daily prayers. Yet, strangely, Jesus did not repeat the prayer verbatim. He added a new phrase, not found in the Hebrew original: "and with all your mind." Jesus both preserves tradition and creates innovation.

What did the Shema mean, and what did Jesus mean? For the ancient Jews, the Shema meant that we were created to live for God. Even though we might feel great love for other people, God requires our greatest love, our whole heart. Jesus' addition to the Shema takes the prayer a step further. The kind of love that God commands from us is not just love from the heart, that is, not just emotional love, but a rational and intellectual love as well, love from the mind.

On this point, as on so many others, Jesus did not go into any sort of explanation. Jesus preferred not to spell it all out for us. In addition to heart, soul, and will (strength), he wanted us to use our minds to love God. And the mind is the home of our capacity to think. Truly loving God in the way that Jesus calls us to requires us to think about God, to become theologians.

What we find here is Jesus taking the Jewish tradition of loving God and modifying it in such a way as to make it deeper and stronger. For Jesus, true faith did not mean simply following the ancient precepts we have received in the Bible. Jesus opposed any sort of religion that blindly followed its scriptures word for word. Blindly following what you may read or what you are told by your Church leader is not "loving God with all your mind." Or to put the matter more strongly, Jesus did not even want us to follow him blindly. He was very careful and consistent not to spell out a "program" for us. His parables and sayings make us think; they do not provide a list of instructions and regulations. Jesus never said that we needed priests or preachers or leaders to tell us what to think and how to live. He told us to love God with our minds, not with someone else's mind.

In this one addition to the ancient Jewish prayer, Jesus pointed toward a whole new way of doing religion. Faith in God, for Jesus, was a matter of the head, not just the heart; it was a matter of love, not just faith. Jesus never wrote a book to explain this for us. He knew that even he was not adequate to the task. Jesus knew God at every level, yet God can reveal God's inexhaustible riches to us in ways not revealed to Jesus. Every one of us, including Jesus, experiences God differently. Jesus may never have known the mystical rapture of St. Teresa of Ávila or St. Hildegard of Bingen. But he would have recognized that they loved God with all their hearts. Jesus never knew the theological depth of thought displayed in the complex writings of Origen, St. Augustine, Paul Tillich, and David Tracy. But he would have known that these people loved God with all their minds. St. Anselm said that God was that which is greater than anything that can be humanly conceived. One of the implications of this "ontological argument" for the existence of God is that we can continually conceive more and more about God, we can know God and love God deeper and deeper with our minds, but we can never know it all. When we strive to deepen our understanding of God with our minds, we enrich our lives with a deeper love of God.

Who Is My Neighbor?

For Jesus, the love commandment did not stop with the Shema, or even with his addition to it. Jesus gave a second commandment in answer to the scribe's question. Jesus' second commandment is not found in any list of what we call the Ten Commandments. He said, "The second is this, 'You shall love your neighbor as yourself.'" This second commandment is taken entirely from Leviticus 19:18, with nothing added by Jesus. What is unique for Jesus is the use he makes of it. Whereas the Shema was the greatest prayer of the Jewish faith, Leviticus 19:18 is a rather obscure passage. Jesus took it from the background and raised it to a place of primary importance.

To be sure, an older rabbi from Jesus' time, the famous Hillel, had likewise seen these two as the greatest commandments of the Torah. But Jesus used this obscure commandment in a slightly different way, and carried its implications considerably further than did Hillel.

In its Levitical context, this commandment is part of a small section urging its readers not to hold grudges or take revenge. It comes within a section of Leviticus that scholars call the "holiness code." Much of the material in it describes things God's people need to do in order to be holy before God. It is in a completely different section, even a different book, than the Shema. Jesus put this obscure passage together with the more famous one to invite a new understanding of the meaning of Torah. The Torah is not just a list of 613 commands from God that God's people must follow to lead good lives and be pleasing to their maker. Rather, Jesus' new Torah takes the Torah's message a step further. These two love commandments become the centerpiece, the lens through which everything else in the Torah, and everything else in human life, must be viewed. Jesus calls his followers to put love above all else and to see everything through the eyes of love. Seeing everything through the eyes of love presents us with the greatest challenge and the most problems.

In Luke's version of this dialogue about the greatest commandment, the questioner pushes Jesus a little further. Regarding the second love commandment, "Love your neighbor as yourself," he asks, "And who is my neighbor?" (10:29). Jesus then proceeds to tell the story of the good Samaritan" (10:30–37). Most of us reading this parable today think of it as a story of how everyone should help out anyone else who is in trouble. This is, however, a rather different lesson from the one Jesus would have expected his listeners to hear.

A man has been robbed and left desolate and wounded by the side of the road. A priest, and later a Levite, pass by the man and do not help him. Jesus' listeners would have considered priests and Levites to be the most morally upright of the Jews, people of high position, well regarded by all, and with considerable means and wealth. They led exemplary lives, and others looked up to them. Samaritans, in contrast, were despised by Jewish society. They had for centuries been considered half-breed mongrels who were not really Jews and not really gentiles. They lived in Samaria, the region between the two Jewish regions of Judea and Galilee. The Jews considered them to be dangerous, and went to great lengths to avoid them.

Jesus' listeners, all of whom were Jews, heard this story quite differently from the way we hear it. From their perspective, a representative of the most despised people the Jews knew of turns out to be the hero. Their good guys, priests and Levites, turn out to be the bad guys; the bad guy turns out to be the good guy.

We should note that this prejudice, like most prejudices, worked both ways. The Samaritans disliked the Jews as much as the Jews disliked them. Most Samaritans would have been quite happy to see a Jew lying wounded in a ditch. If Jesus had told this story to a group of Samaritans, they probably would have disliked it just as much as the Jews to whom he did tell it.

We could, of course, rename the characters and put the story in a modern context. For me, growing up in the segregated South in the 1950s, the story could have been titled "The Good African-American." For a present-day Palestinian Arab, it would be "The Good Jew." Or for a present-day Israeli Jew, it would be "The Good Arab." For many American Christians these days, the story might be titled "The Good Muslim." The hearer of the story in all cases is challenged to see his or her chosen "enemy" in a different light.

As we have seen again and again, Jesus, in words and actions, advocated against all prejudices. He never spoke negatively about Samaritans, gentiles in general, or the Roman occupying forces in particular. The only people Jesus ever spoke against were some of his own people, most often the Pharisees, to whom he was actually very close in both his thinking and his actions. All his arguments with them occurred within his own group. He never criticized any Jewish group or individual to any non-Jews.

So we return now to the lawyer's question, "Who is my neighbor?" Jesus' answer is that our neighbor is that person or group against whom we have the most prejudice, the person or group whom we most dislike. And Jesus' instruction for how we should deal with these most feared, hated, disliked, and despised people is that we are to love them. That love needs to be more than an abstract statement of principle, more than just *saying* that we love them. It needs to be love shown in action, just as the good Samaritan acted to help the wounded Jew to full recovery.

Love to the Extreme

Jesus makes his call for extreme love most emphatically in the Sermon on the Mount. The Sermon on the Mount is constantly quoted and praised by Christians, but it contains some of the most consistently ignored teachings of Jesus. For example, Jesus states in a more direct, concise, and one could even say, radical form what he has said in the parable of the good Samaritan:

> "You have heard that it was said, 'You shall love your neighbor and hate your enemy.' But I say to you, Love your enemies and pray for those who persecute you" (Matt. 5:43–44).

We have noted that the idea of loving your neighbor is found in the Torah of the Hebrew Scriptures, in Leviticus 19:18. Jesus' story of the good Samaritan defined *neighbor,* much to the chagrin of Jesus' hearers, as people from the group that you most dislike. Readers might assume that the phrase "hate your enemy," used by Jesus in the Sermon on the Mount, is from the same Old Testament quotation. It is not. Although the Old Testament tells us to love our neighbors, it does not tell us to hate our enemies. Over the years, or even centuries, people apparently added the phrase "hate your enemy" as a corollary of "love your neighbor." This addition became so widespread that people began to think it was scriptural. Jesus quickly and clearly dispels that notion, and then makes the statement that pushes love to the extreme, "Love your enemies and pray for those who persecute you."

The idea of loving your enemies is not completely absent from the Old Testament. In Proverbs 25:21–22 we read:

> If your enemies are hungry, give them bread to eat;
> and if they are thirsty, give them water to drink;
> for you will heap coals of fire on their heads,
> and the Lord will reward you.

In the New Testament, Paul quotes this verse approvingly in Romans 12:20. But Jesus goes much further than either Proverbs or Paul. Proverbs and Paul are seeing love as a kind of ironic vengeance. This kind of love, given to one's enemy, will not be received as love but as a weird form of punishment. Jesus, to the contrary, was calling for genuine love for one's enemies, the *agape* love that gives without any expectation of return, and certainly not with the expectation that the love will be received as ironic punishment. When Jesus said, "Love your enemies," he really meant for us to love our enemies.

The practice of nonviolence is also taught in the Sermon on the Mount:

> "You have heard that it was said, 'An eye for an eye and a tooth for a tooth.' But I say to you, Do not resist an evildoer. But if anyone strikes you on the right cheek, turn the other also" (Matt. 5:38–39).

The early Christians took Jesus at his word and practiced nonviolence in all their dealings with the Roman Empire, despite numerous persecutions. The Roman army particularly disliked the Christians and would not allow them into the army. They feared that Christians would not fight in battle but would go over to the enemy and try to tell them about Jesus Christ. Perhaps the greatest miracle that ever occurred, greater than any miracle in the Bible, is that the Christians were able eventually to defeat the Roman Empire, the most powerful empire that had ever ruled the earth—and without ever raising the sword. The Christians defeated the Romans not with violence but with love. In the year 313, through an edict of the Emperor Constantine, whose mother, Helena, was a Christian, Christianity became a legal religion in the Roman Empire. Three centuries of persecution came to an end. Love works. Loving your enemies works. Turning the other cheek works. The early Christians did not think that the love Jesus called for was an impractical ideal to strive for in an all-too-violent world. They believed that Jesus said what he meant. They followed his love commandment fully, and eventually love triumphed.

Unfortunately, almost as soon as Christian love triumphed, it was abandoned. Once Christians gained political power in the Roman Empire, they began to wield the sword. Christians have been violent ever since. The Crusades in the Middle Ages, the Spanish Inquisition, and Christian persecution of Jews throughout the centuries are among the worst examples. To this day Christians justify violence in the name of him who taught precisely the opposite.

The first Christian since the fourth century to effectively question Christian use of violence was Dr. Martin Luther King Jr. He saw, in the work of Mahatma Gandhi, the effectiveness of nonviolence as a means to social change. Although Gandhi was a Hindu and not a Christian, King saw no conflicts between the principles of Gandhi and the principles of Jesus Christ in the matter of nonviolence. Because he was in theological school in Boston at the time, King did not actually begin the civil rights movement, but he soon became its leader. He carried the campaign forward with brilliant oratory that moved masses of people to change the direction of their thinking. He used superb organizational skills, developed tactics of civil disobedience, and maintained a principle of nonviolence and love throughout his mission. He carried his work to other major issues of the day, most notably in his opposition to the Vietnam War. Through it all King maintained an attitude of Christian love, *agape*, toward even the worst of his enemies. Through it all he never committed one violent act, and he made sure, to the best of his ability, that none of his followers used violence. Like Gandhi and Jesus, he died a violent death.

But nonviolence worked. Love worked. The civil rights struggle was won. Though the kind of complete respect, freedom, and love between the races that Dr. King envisioned has yet to be achieved, the struggle to eliminate discrimination from the law and the enforcement of the law has essentially been achieved. Having grown up in the segregated South, I am aware that it is hard for young people today to understand how bad things were for African Americans in the South before the civil rights movement. I remember segregated restrooms and water fountains. I remember how movie theaters relegated blacks to the non-air-conditioned third balcony, which could be reached only by climbing an outside fire escape. I remember the preaching of racism in the pulpits and Sunday schools of my segregated Methodist Church.

But I also remember one incredibly brave young director of Christian education at my church. Susan Lutz Allred was twenty-three years old and fresh out of college when she began working at my church. Within a few months, she had invited a choir from a local black church to sing at one of our services. The high quality of the music was irrelevant to the members of the church who vehemently opposed the visit, owing only to the race of the singers. It is a wonder that Susan was able to keep her job. But somehow, through her steady perseverance, her godly innocence that always saw the best in people and ignored the worst, her cheerful personality, her right and just cause, and her abounding Christian love, Susan kept her job. She brought in other black singers and speakers over the course of the years. They and she changed the thinking and the lives of many of our church members, especially the youth. Like Dr. King and Jesus, she did it all with love.

Coming through college in an era when women did not enter ordained ministry, Susan took the route that was open to her: Christian education. Several years later, when women were beginning to be received more readily into the ministry of the United Methodist Church, she went back to divinity school, was ordained, and became a parish minister. For several years now, she has been the pastor of one of the most significant churches in North Carolina, Aldersgate United Methodist in Chapel Hill.

Great examples of the followers of Jesus, from Dr. King to Mother Teresa to John Paul II to Susan Lutz Allred, have all understood one thing: love works. Those who have followed Jesus have found that the hardest lesson he ever taught, love your enemies, ultimately works.

Taking Love of Enemies One Short Step Further

Jesus did not seek out controversy, nor did he avoid it. At times he pushed things to the limit, most notably when he turned over the tables of the money changers and the sellers of sacrificial animals in the temple courtyard in Jerusalem (Mark 11:15–19). Jesus did not try to make enemies, but enemies arose nonetheless. Jesus tried only to recruit people for the Kingdom of God, but the Kingdom of God has always had its enemies. For some in Jesus' time, the kingdom of the Romans was the greatest kingdom they could ever want or imagine. They did not understand the Kingdom of God, nor did they want to understand it. Today the temptations of our secular kingdoms, with all their wealth and power, lead many away from the Kingdom of God. Most simply ignore the Kingdom of God, but some become its enemies.

Jesus had no lack of enemies to love and pray for. For him, for Martin Luther King Jr., and for many other Christian leaders, enemies are unavoidable. Most of us, however, have another option: we can avoid making enemies. In the Sermon on the Mount, Jesus gave us a simple rule to follow: "In everything do to others as you would have them do to you" (Matt. 7:12). If we practice this aptly termed Golden Rule, we are sure to make fewer enemies than if we don't practice it.

For whatever reason, some among us seem to be more naturally loving than others; to some the Golden Rule comes more easily. Perhaps the most naturally loving person I have ever met is a man I knew in college named George Goodrich. His last name was remarkably apropos. His nickname was Goody. George was one of those people who did all manner of good things for others without being asked. So many of them were little things that people scarcely noticed. A friend told me about something George did when he was a hurdler on the track team in college. George noticed that the student who was the team manager had more work than he could reasonably get done in the amount of time he had, so George would always arrive at practice early and set up the hurdles. After practice George would stay late and return the hurdles to their place in the gym.

George always found time to help others. In those days before computers, getting last-minute term papers typed was a common need. Students could go to the typing bureau, but that not only cost money, it was not available during the wee hours of the morning when students most needed it. George spent a lot of hours on a lot of nights typing term papers for others, even friends of friends, and he never charged for it. He typed one for me once. He also inspired me to type a few for others. George always got his own work done early, purposely, so he would have time to do work for others. Although he was a fine student, I suspect he would have had higher grades if he had devoted to himself all the time he spent helping others.

George was a practitioner of, in the words of a bumper sticker slogan, "random acts of kindness." He never discussed his good deeds; he just did them. They came naturally to him. What George did tell people about, when the occasion presented itself, was the love of Jesus Christ. Since college, I haven't kept up with George. I have heard that he is a minister of a church in New Jersey or Pennsylvania.

Being good and doing good came easily to George. He found it almost impossible to make enemies. Being good and doing good comes less naturally to most of us. For some of us, it is difficult indeed. I think I am fairly average at being good. I would like to think that I get better as I get older, though I recognize that this may be wishful thinking. I have no secret formulas for being good, no ten-step program to goodness. Most of the things I might say to instruct people in the way of goodness are things everyone would already know (though not necessarily do).

Let me offer just one possibility for greater goodness. Try to do one good thing each week—beyond anything you would normally do. It does not have to be planned. It does not need to be time-consuming. It could be a small as picking up a piece of trash on the sidewalk and carrying it to a proper receptacle. It could be something, or many things, that are much bigger. Just do it. You do not need to tell anyone about it.

LOVE IS STRONGER THAN SIN

A seventeenth-century French monk known as Brother Lawrence wrote a remarkable book called *The Practice of the Presence of God.* His title is an apt description of what we call spirituality. Given that God is present in all aspects of our lives, it follows that spirituality is various and manifold. It can be as standardized as the practice of saying the Lord's Prayer or celebrating the Eucharist. It can be as individualized as each person's special way of being in God's presence. The unifying factors are God's love for humanity and humanity's love for God.

My spirituality was first awakened in the early seventies, when I was in graduate school. I began attending an evangelically oriented Presbyterian church near campus. The membership included lots of students. The sermons were expositions of biblical passages with an eye toward practical application in daily life. There was much emphasis on prayer, including small prayer groups. The membership displayed a spiritual hunger of a sort I had not previously encountered. They also displayed bonds of deep love both for God and for one another. The church nourished me for two-and-a-half years. I even became a part-time assistant pastor and preached there several times. The presence of genuine *agape* was tangible in this church. Yet over the course of time, the differences between their beliefs and mine became clearer to me. I had hoped to have a liberalizing effect on them insofar as biblical interpretation was concerned. Although the pastor could not be classified as a fundamentalist, many of the church members could be. More and more I found that the kind of historical, critical biblical study that engaged me in my doctoral program conflicted with the noncritical attitudes toward the Bible held by most of the church members, who seemed never to permit themselves a critical or historical thought about a biblical text or a church doctrine.

Moreover, I discovered during the time I spent in this evangelical Presbyterian Church that I was not just a Christian, I was a United Methodist Christian. My tradition, which stems from Methodist founder John Wesley, has some fundamentally different viewpoints from the tradition of John Calvin, whose influence was clear in the thinking of the Presbyterian church members and pastor.

Specifically, John Calvin considered humanity to be "utterly depraved" and fully deserving of eternal punishment. He believed that God had decided, from before the beginning of time, to save a few people, who are saved only by God's grace, not through any works of their own. The marks of their salvation are their membership in an evangelical church, their honesty and loyalty, their diligence and prosperity, and their conservative attitudes in virtually all social and political matters. They have a low view of humanity and the world—humans are on the whole a bad lot, and the world is essentially an evil place whose time is limited.

John Wesley had a different view. Wesley's most distinctive contribution to the history of Christian theology was his doctrine of perfection. Wesley took his cue from Jesus in the Sermon on the Mount: "Be perfect, therefore, as your heavenly Father is perfect" (Matt. 5:48). Wesley developed the idea that Christians, far from being utterly depraved, were going on to perfection and could be expected to be made perfect in love in this life.

When I was ordained into the United Methodist ministry, I had to answer thirty-eight questions. Wesley had asked these same questions of the preachers he commissioned in the eighteenth century. Two of the questions gave me pause: "Are you going on to perfection?" and "Do you expect to be made perfect in love in this life?" A Calvinist could not answer these questions affirmatively; nor could, I suspect, most Lutherans and many members of other denominations. I could, and did, answer in the affirmative. I was not sure that I believed my answers, and I expected that even though I had been instructed about the Wesleyan meaning of these questions, there was more to them than I realized. I am still realizing their deeper meaning.

It is often said that you can use the Bible to prove any point you want to make. Certainly one can emphasize certain Bible passages to the exclusion of others in order to make a theological point more forcefully. Is the Calvinist low view of humanity and the world correct? Or is the Wesleyan high view better? Or is it something in between, more like a Lutheran view? One of the classic texts for the low view of humanity is Psalm 51:1–5, written in the context of David's affair with Bathsheba. We discussed this psalm earlier, specifically as a proof-text for the doctrine of original sin. The psalmist expresses a low view of himself throughout the psalm, climaxing in, "Indeed, I was born guilty, a sinner when my mother conceived me" (v. 5).

Psalm 51 may beautifully express an individual's feelings at a low time in his life, but nothing in the psalm indicates that it is applicable to all human beings or should be the foundation of a principle Christian doctrine of a low view of humankind. When generalized to all humanity, the psalm implies that we, because of our innate sinfulness, are incapable of true *agape*. Only God has mercy. Only God can truly love. When God loves, it is only by the good fortune of his grace toward chosen individuals, chosen by criteria known to God alone. All others are judged harshly and are thoroughly deserving of the torments of hell. The chosen, the elect, likewise merit eternal damnation, but God in God's grace has for whatever reason mercifully chosen to save a few.

Although the psalm does not quite say all this, Calvin and others pulled as much from the psalm, and, along with a good dose of Paul's writings interpreted in the same context, created a low view of humanity and the world. I would contend that this low view is not the predominant biblical view.

After each day of creation, according to the Genesis creation story, "God saw that it was good" (1:4, 10, 12, 18, 21, 25, 31). Moreover, when God created humankind, "God blessed them" (1:28). Before any word of sin enters the story, God recognizes creation as good—again and again—and blesses humankind.

Many Christians will say that the sin of Adam and Eve negates the blessing. The Bible never says this. Sinfulness *is* part of the human condition; but it is not an inherited part of the human condition. It can be overcome. Whatever our human propensity for sin, we are made in the image of God. Temptation can be resisted. The only force in the universe that is irresistible is the overwhelming love of God.

God did not create us to be utterly depraved, miserable sinners in the mold of the speaker of Psalm 51. A much more accurate expression of God's intent for humanity is found in another psalm:

> When I look at your heavens, the work of your fingers,
> the moon and the stars that you have established;
> what are human beings that you are mindful of them,
> mortals that you care for them?
>
> Yet you have made them a little lower than God,
> and crowned them with glory and honor.
> You have given them dominion over the works of your hands;
> you have put all things under their feet (8:3–6).

The statement, "Yet you have made them a little lower than God," was so shocking in its implications for the nature of humanity that early transcribers and translators changed the word *God* to "angels" or "divine beings." Yet the psalm really says that we humans are but a little lower than God. This psalm, furthermore, addresses the nature of humanity, not just one individual person. Recall that Psalm 51 is set in the context of one specific person, David, in reference to his sin with Bathsheba. The Christian Church has tended to make of Psalm 51 a general statement about humanity. Psalm 8, on the other hand, makes a clear statement about humanity, yet the tendency of the Church has been to ignore it.

The implications of Psalm 8 are clear and straightforward, as are the implications of the Genesis creation story. Created in the image of God, we are crowned with honor and glory. God thinks no less of us for our sin. God has high expectations for humanity. God is perfect in love, for "God is love" (1 John 4:8), and we are created in God's image. God's love is marked all over us. Jesus called us to perfection. We need merely to allow God's image to shine out from us. When we let the love within shine forth, we know the greatest pleasure.

JESUS AND ROMANTIC LOVE

The Old Testament abounds with stories of romantic love, but the New Testament in general, and the Gospels in particular, seem deficient in this regard. Although romantic love has been the principal subject of most of our songs and stories throughout the ages, Jesus had virtually nothing to say about it. What few things he did say were not among his most profound utterances, but they do shed light on the character of a truly Christian approach to romantic love.

"But from the beginning of creation, 'God made them male and female.' 'For this reason a man shall leave his father and mother and be joined to his wife, and the two shall become one flesh.' . . . Therefore what God has joined together, let no one separate" (Mark 10:6–9).

Jesus clearly blessed the institution of marriage. He blessed it not only with these words but also with his actions at the wedding feast in Cana of Galilee, where he turned the water into wine. Yet Jesus himself never married. He enjoyed the company of many women throughout the course of his ministry, but the Gospels record no expression or display of romantic feelings for any of them. We might surmise that the woman in Luke 7:37–50, who anointed and kissed Jesus' feet, may have had some romantic feelings toward him. We may surmise that Mary Magdalene, who followed him from Galilee to Jerusalem, who was the last at the cross and the first at the tomb, had some feelings of love for him. We may suppose that had he lived a longer life, Jesus might eventually have married and had a family, for certainly that was his advice to others. But Jesus had no experience and little advice on the two deepest human loves we can experience: love of a man or a woman, and love of our children. The best we can do, and perhaps it is good enough, is to apply the qualities of love we see in Jesus' relationships with others, and what he says about love in general, to our own love for our mates and our children.

The utter self-givingness of *agape*, as described by Paul in 1 Corinthians, chapter 13, can lead us into the deepest pleasures of romantic love. The intensity of love in romance is far more than the chemistry of attraction. When we read the great love stories—Jacob and Rachel in the Bible, Daphnis and Chloe in classical literature, Romeo and Juliet in Shakespeare, or Heathcliff and Catherine in Emily Brontë's *Wuthering Heights*—the central themes of romantic love emerge from all of them. The lover gives part of his or her identity to the beloved and takes part of the beloved's identity for himself or herself. The two become lost in each other, and in their lostness find a new level of identity. In Jesus' words, the two become one flesh. It may reach a level of passionate intensity in the act of lovemaking, when the two literally become one flesh. Or it may be something much less intense and far more subtle, but no less loving. The touch of a hand on a shoulder, the glance of knowing eyes that meet for an instant, a sweet sound in the voice as the beloved's name is spoken—we who love or have loved know these moments. "You have ravished my heart with a glance of your eyes," says the Song of Songs (4:9).

The pleasure of romantic love is enhanced when a couple has shared interests and experiences, something more than a sexual attraction or familial bonds. When that couple in love have been together for a long time, they develop a history of shared experiences, of times and places and events that belong only to them and that help define their identity as a couple. Some of these most treasured memories that we have as a couple may be of things that did not seem spectacular or wonderful at the time, just deeply good. In memory, the depth of that goodness is enhanced.

For Marianne, my wife, and me, the best of those memories are almost entirely away from work and home, in travels both near and far. We spent four days, for example, in Sorrento, Italy, in 1991. In the beautiful hotel, our balcony overlooked the Bay of Naples, with the Isle of Capri on the left and Mt. Vesuvius on the right. We spent a day on Capri and a day at Pompeii and Mt. Vesuvius. We took a bus trip down the incredibly beautiful Amalfi Coast, where every turn of the somewhat harrowing mountain road yields a view more spectacular than the last of the brilliant blue Mediterranean strewn with steep volcanic isles. We spent the afternoon in the astounding city of Positano, a city built down the side of a mountain, its houses seeming to hang precipitously over the sea. In the evening, after elegant dinners in the hotel's dining room, we strolled the town square of Sorrento, sipped cappuccino at sidewalk cafes, and listened to Italian popular music.

We share memories from closer to home, in particular from Ocracoke Island in the North Carolina Outer Banks. This wild and ruggedly beautiful ribbon of sand and sea has fourteen miles of totally undeveloped beach—not a house or building in sight. The southern tip of the island has a small village with a gorgeous harbor and not a single chain store or fast-food place. The native old-timers who sit on the porch of the general store still have a strange accent with vague sounds of England, left over from the island's three hundred years of isolation since the pirate Edward Teach, better known as Blackbeard, made his headquarters there.

One perfect day, we walked along the beach at low tide. As we splashed through the soft sand at surf's edge, we both suddenly felt tiny shellfish streaming around our toes. We looked down to see thousands of the smallest shells in myriad bright and beautiful colors. We had discovered coquinas. We got on our hands and knees in the surf and sifted hundreds of coquinas through our fingers, marveling at their loveliness. They came in virtually every color: bright yellows, blues, whites, oranges, purples, and browns, with a few that were dark greenish and deep reddish. Most were one color. Some were striped. The little shells made a glistening rainbow in the sunlit surf and sand.

Marianne and I were like children in our sense of wonder at these little bits of newly discovered beauty in God's creation.

Now when we are at Ocracoke, we sometimes see adults and children on their knees, sifting sand through their fingers with the same sense of wonder at their own discovery of these lovely little creatures. The wonder has never left. We still love to look at these creatures to this day, but one of our most treasured memories as a couple was the day we first discovered them.

Jesus often noted the beauty of nature around him as he traversed the Galilee. The little things of nature became subjects for his parables. He saw the beauty in the lilies of the field and the birds of the air. He noted for us the care that God took with creation. Jesus did not have enough years to amass the memories that couples form their lives of love upon. But Jesus had an eye for what is lovely and a heart for what is the pleasure of love.

Unlike Jesus, most of us do find a loving mate with whom to share our lives. For those of us who have found that lifelong mate, the passion of *eros* can remain undiminished, even as *agape* endlessly grows. The essence of all love is giving. Jesus gave love unending. We give what we have, and when we give it, we know the greatest pleasure.

JESUS AND THE LOVE OF CHILDREN

Jesus was never a parent. Children play a remarkably small role in the stories of Jesus in the Gospels. We have but a single story of Jesus' own childhood, Luke's account (2:41–52) of Jesus, at age twelve, in the Jerusalem temple. We do not hear of the children of any of Jesus' disciples. Although Jesus' healings occasionally include children, the children are always passive recipients of his healing, the parents taking the more active roles. The Gospels contain no stories in which individual children are identified by name. One story, however, shows Jesus' love for children:

> People were bringing little children to him in order that he might touch them; and the disciples spoke sternly to them. But when Jesus saw this, he was indignant and said to them, "Let the little children come to me; do not stop them; for it is to such as these that the kingdom of God belongs. Truly I tell you, whoever does not receive the kingdom of God as a little child will never enter it." And he took them up in his arms, laid his hands on them, and blessed them (Mark 10:13–16).

Were it not for this one story, whose major point is something other than the love of children, we would not know that Jesus cared for children at all.

The point of the story is that one must receive the Kingdom of God as would a child. Though thousands of sermons have been preached on this topic, Jesus does not really spell out what he means by this. If we are to gather our interpretations from the context of the other parables of the Kingdom of heaven, we are probably right in concluding that Jesus means one must receive the Kingdom with a child's innocent sense of wonder. It is like the coquina shells squishing through the sand under our feet on the beach. They may first escape our notice, but when we do see them and see how beautiful they are, we are filled with awe and wonder. Having a sense of wonder is one of the greatest things about being a child.

Though the main point of the story is about receiving the Kingdom of God, what is most important for us in this study is Jesus' love of the children. The Gospels show that Jesus sometimes had the problem of large crowds pressing too closely, as when he healed the woman with the twelve-year flow of blood. In this story, parents are bringing their children close to Jesus so that they might touch him. We are not told why. Perhaps some of the children were sick, and the parents sought healing. Other parents may have wanted their children to touch this man who, perhaps, would one day be known as one of the greatest rabbis of the Galilee. Doubtless none of them actually knew the true measure of his greatness.

The disciples had seen the crowds around Jesus grow in number, up to around five thousand for the miracle of the loaves and fishes a few chapters earlier in Mark. They were aware of the potential for Jesus being hurt, accidentally or intentionally, in the midst of a crowd. When the crowd of children and parents pressed in on him, the disciples grew concerned. Jesus, on the other hand, looked at the situation as an opportunity to indulge himself in a pleasure he rarely enjoyed, the pleasure of children. Merely to hold a child in one's arms, to feel the love and trust and warmth that can come from a little child, is one of life's fine pleasures. Jesus blessed these little children. He apparently took the time to bless each child individually. In his so doing, we feel his blessing for every child everywhere.

Children are our blessing. Our children are our greatest love. The bond between a parent and a child is the strongest form of love we know. Jesus once said that there is no greater love than giving up one's life for another. We have that great a love for our children. Our love for our children is the most self-giving love we ever experience. It is the kind of love that comes closest to the pure *agape* of God (it is perhaps no accident that the image of God as parent was favored by Jesus). It is the kind of love that comes closest to the love that Jesus showed for humanity in his life and in his death.

Marianne and I have been blessed with two wonderful children who have given us maximal blessing with minimal problems. I have never been called on to risk my life, or even to risk serious injury, for my children. I have no heroic personal stories to tell. Yet one vignette of parental love stands out in my mind, at least at this moment.

We were on a family weekend vacation at the beach. My daughter, April, perhaps eleven at the time, had been to writing camp the previous summer. She had long kept a personal journal. She had brought the journal to the beach that day and had written in it, in between times of swimming, walking, and reading.

Suddenly a storm arose. All four of us gathered our belongings quickly and made our way to the car to drive back to the hotel. We had driven only a short distance when a torrential downpour made it almost impossible for me to see through the windshield. At that moment April remembered and told us that she had left her journal at the beach. I knew how important her journal was to her and that it would ruin her vacation if it were lost. Still, she did not expect that I would make an effort to rescue it. I did not expect to be able to rescue it. Even if we turned around and went back to the beach, the journal would probably have blown away in the howling winds. Even if I found it, it would surely have been soaked beyond legibility. Yet for some parental-love sort of reason, I knew I had to try.

I turned the car around in the driving rainstorm. Neither Marianne nor our son, John, objected. Both knew that under the same circumstances they would want me to do the same thing for them. We drove the two miles or so back to the beach. When we arrived, to our astonishment the rain had not yet hit there. I got out of the car and ran as fast as I could to the abandoned beach. (I should note that after three back operations, I had not run, at all, in several years, and have not run since.) Thunder pounded over me and lightning flashed too close for comfort. I found the journal on the beach exactly where April had left it. I grabbed it and ran back to the car as fast as I could. John had followed me and retrieved a couple of other items we had left on the beach. The rain hit just as soon as we got back in the car. The journal was dry.

I remember the look in April's eyes when I gave her the journal. She knew the joy of having recovered intact something important to her that she was sure had been lost forever. She also knew that I loved her very much. Exhausted but delighted, I was amazed at the recovery. It felt wonderful to be my daughter's hero.

OUR GREAT PLEASURE

The deepest lesson of the Bible is love. Love is what we know of God. Love is a part of our human nature. People who do not know about Jesus know about love and experience love. But Jesus teaches us more. Jesus teaches us to extend the love that is in our very nature beyond its natural bounds. Jesus teaches us that all too difficult lesson of loving our enemies. It is an abundance of love in our lives that enables us to extend that love to an ever-widening circle. Jesus' love had the widest circle of all—it incorporated everyone. He believed that we could love as greatly as he did.

8 / JESUS AND THE GOOD LIFE

The phrase "the good life" has titled two books I have read recently, one ancient and one current. Cicero, the prolific Roman lawyer, politician, orator, and occasional philosopher, who lived in the first century B.C.E., wrote a book with this title. Cicero's religion consisted of a minimal belief in the gods of Greco-Roman polytheism—a pantheon that, in Cicero's time, functioned more as a civil religion than as a system of faith. Cicero wrote primarily about ethics. Characteristics of his good life included honesty, care, love, appreciation for family, patriotism, courage and duty in the military, and a sense of one's place in the order of society. It was a highly conservative view. Cicero was himself a member of the patrician class, the highest class in a rigidly ordered class system.

In 2002 Peter Gomes, the minister of the Memorial Chapel at Harvard University, and effectively the chaplain of Harvard, wrote a book of the same title. Gomes, too, would, for the most part, be considered conservative in his values. He is a hard-working Yankee Republican with a deep sense of New

England pride of heritage, but he breaks the conservative stereotype in that he is African American, and he is gay. It was my good fortune to have lunch with Peter Gomes the day that he preached the baccalaureate service at my university. A man of great wit and personal charm, Gomes went on that afternoon to give the best baccalaureate I had ever heard.

For Gomes, like Cicero, the idea of the good life focuses on an ethic of discipline, hard work, close family ties, and pride of country, region, and race. While many of Gomes's characteristics of the good life are similar to Cicero's, Gomes himself being well read in classical literature, there is one essential difference between the two. Cicero's ideal society had a rigidly hierarchical class structure, including a massive slave class. Gomes's ideal society, though perhaps not entirely classless, is egalitarian. Everyone in Gomes's society, regardless of socioeconomic background, should have equal opportunity to succeed. Jesus and the entire Christian tradition undergird Gomes's beliefs, as do Martin Luther King Jr. and the American civil rights struggle. Gomes's book draws on his own experience and that of many famous people, and although it is not organized in a systematic fashion, it is a good read, informative and thought provoking.

For both Cicero and Gomes, the good life is essentially an ethical and moral good life, a life of doing good for others. The enjoyment of the pleasures of life is not a matter of high interest for them. I do not for a moment deny the importance of ethical and moral good living, but my understanding of what constitutes the good life is somewhat different.

CHARACTERISTICS OF THE GOOD LIFE

The good life is rooted in the enjoyment of fine pleasures. It is rooted in an aesthetic sense of beauty and a deep yearning for truth. These two, beauty and truth, are completely compatible. As John Keats said in his last lines of "Ode on a Grecian Urn":

> "Beauty is truth, truth beauty,—that is all
> Ye know on earth, and all ye need to know."

Beauty and truth are all around us. They are essential elements of a meaningful life. Beauty and truth can be simple enough to be readily understood by a small child. A loving glance, a burst of blossoms, a sweet song, or coquinas on a beach require no special sophistication to be appreciated, especially on the level of the senses and the emotions. Other aspects of beauty and truth may require study and research for anything that even approaches a full understanding. Far too many beautiful things exist in this universe for any one of us to appreciate them all. I know scholars who are brilliant in their fields but who know scarcely a note of classical music; they have never learned to hear the depth, complexity, and sheer beauty of a Bach fugue or a Puccini aria. I know classical musicians who never go to a concert unless they are playing in it. They know the music on a technical level that I do not, but I am not sure to what extent they feel the music and know its true pleasure.

There are people who create beauty every day, scarcely noticed by any larger public than their own family. Marianne, my wife, does wonderful things with a needle and thread. Besides making beautiful clothes inexpensively, she creates home furnishings so finely done as to startle first-time guests in our home. Yet the craft or art of fine sewing is in decline, at least in this country. What used to be a skill passed on from mother to daughter and taught at more advanced levels in high school and college home-economics courses, now seems to have fallen as a vestige of patriarchy. Now we only buy clothes off the rack and home furnishings ready-made. I was utterly unaware of the intricacy, delicacy, and beauty of cloth finely woven and sewn until I knew Marianne. Though I will never be able to sew a stitch, she has opened up to me this whole realm of beauty and pleasure to the eye.

SEEING AND DOING

In matters of aesthetics, I am in general an observer rather than a participant. My aesthetic pleasure is rarely derived from technical expertise. I deeply love classical music, and many other kinds of music as well, but I neither sing nor play any musical instrument. I can read nine languages, but music is not one of them. I can identify by ear something close to three thousand classical works, but I can tell you very little about the technical structure of any of them. I think that my feeling for music is at a deep level, but it is a different level from someone who plays music. When I watch the intensity with which someone like Pamela Frank or Joshua Bell plays the violin, I know that they are feeling the music at a deeper level than I ever will. Nonetheless, though I may not create the pleasure, I in some sense know it.

Not since I made a D in second-grade art have I seriously tried to draw a picture. I learned virtually nothing about art in high school. When I came to college, I wanted to learn at least something about great art and what made it great. I took two art history courses, both of which were taught by mediocre professors. But I needed no teacher to inspire me. The classes revolved around pictures of great works of art flashing on a movie screen while the professor droned on about the images and the artists. In the darkened room, I suspect that sleep was the normal behavior of most of the students. I was fascinated. The final exam required us to identify at sight more than eight hundred works of art, some by only a detailed piece of the painting. For most of the students, study for the final was drudgery; for me, it was joy. My home is now filled with art books, and I have visited most of the great museums of the world. I love art from virtually every period and in virtually every style. Yet I still cannot paint a stroke. Some of the artists I know have less knowledge of art history than I do. Their pleasure in art occurs on a different level than mine.

I have many friends who find pleasure in the game of golf. It is a fascinating, historic, and wonderful game—an exceedingly complex game that has its own aesthetic. Novelist John Updike has written quite a bit about golf, a game to which he is passionately devoted. I remember one of his characters speaking of the aesthetic beauty of a perfectly lofted seven-iron shot, the ball suspended high above the earth for a seemingly endless time, until it finally descends ever so gently, landing softly on the green. Every golfer knows the pleasure of such moments.

I have played golf, with a few years out for back operations, since I was sixteen. Playing it has rarely been a pleasure for me. Despite several instructors, many lessons, much practice, and considerable investment in good equipment, I am still a dreadfully awful golfer. Golf is frustrating, embarrassing, and stressful for me. The single most stressful point comes when I have to drive off the first tee, especially if other people are waiting for and watching me.

I still play about twice a year, just to keep my hand in it. I try to pick days when the weather forecast is bad, so that I may not have to finish the whole round, and so there will be few other golfers on the course. I prefer to play alone. This works out well, because I am rarely if ever invited to play with others! Although each round is a semiannual exercise in frustration, once in a while I have a good moment. Those rare moments come when I am the only person within sight on the course. In those moments I am with God and nature and no one else. I become relaxed. I usually start to hit the ball better. For those few moments, I realize why golf brings so much pleasure to so many people.

Would Jesus have been a golfer? If the game existed during his time, it would probably have been reserved for the Roman occupying army (Roman soldiers loved to play games) and the wealthier Jews. Jesus, being lower on the socioeconomic ladder, would not have gotten a chance to play. Perhaps the more relevant question is whether, if he lived today, Jesus would be a golfer. All golfers would doubtless say yes. Most non-golfers would say no.

The thing to remember is that Jesus was not an ascetic. Jesus loved the pleasures of this life. We live in an era when there are far more pleasures to be enjoyed than Jesus ever knew about. Jesus appreciated the good things in life, and wanted all aspects of the good life for everyone, not just the few who were rich. I believe that Jesus would have heartily approved of golf and all the other sports and recreational activities that give us pleasure and bring no harm. I suspect that Jesus' only objection would be the cost of greens and cart fees.

Although I am for the most part a spectator of the pleasures of life, an observer rather than a doer, I have recently, along with my wife, become engaged in an activity in which observing is doing. We have become bird-watchers, or birders, a word I like less but which seems to have become the current nomenclature. Because we spend most of our summertime in the Outer Banks of North Carolina, I have become particularly interested in shorebirds. Brown pelicans, great white egrets, blue herons, white ibises, and scores of other shorebirds abound in this area. On an organized bird outing this past summer, we had close-up looks at a great white egret, a snowy egret, and ospreys. We also explored a nature trail with a boardwalk through the marine forest, where we saw a beautiful view of the Pamlico Sound, as well as more birds—including a green heron and a tricolored heron—and butterflies (and of course that most ubiquitous of all marine life forms, the mosquito). It was a good trip, a piece of the good life.

A week later we went for another guided birding tour at the Pea Island National Wildlife Refuge on Hatteras Island. This refuge had scores of beautiful bird species, not hidden in a forest but all out front in enormous shallow water flats filled with the things shorebirds love to eat. Our guide, an old-time environmental lawyer who volunteered to lead tours once a week, was incredibly knowledgeable. He could recognize all the songbirds by their calls. He had a spotting scope that he could quickly and expertly train on a particular species so that each of us could look at it up close and see its distinctive features. I have a particular interest in terns. He showed me, through the scope, seven different species of terns, and pointed out their differences and distinctive markings. He showed us some large white birds, which we thought were great egrets but which were actually immature blue herons. We looked at the amazing black skimmer, which, instead of wading and poking its bill to get small fish, crabs, and other bottom dwellers, flies just above the water, skimming the surface with its lower jaw. Its amazing digestive system takes in and filters out masses of salt water to find small, edible creatures. In two and a half hours, we saw more than forty species of shorebirds. Even if I had brought pen and notebook, I don't think I would have had time to note them all.

Jesus was a bird watcher. He did not have a scope or binoculars. He did not have a field guide with pictures of all the species in their different annual plumage. He did, however, see the birds and appreciate their beauty as part of God's creation. He even used birds to illustrate points about human life:

> "Therefore I tell you, do not worry about your life, what you will eat or what you will drink, or about your body, what you will wear. Is not life more than food, and the body more than clothing? Look at the birds of the air; they neither sow nor reap nor gather into barns, and yet your heavenly Father feeds them. Are you not of more value than they?" (Matt. 6:25–26).

Jesus marveled not only at the beauty of the birds but at their spontaneity, their independence, and their abilities. The English romantic poet Percy Shelley captures the deep pleasure that I, and I suspect, Jesus, found in watching birds, in his ode "To a Skylark." The poem begins:

> Hail to thee, blithe spirit!
> Bird thou never wert,
> That from Heaven, or near it,
> Pourest thy full heart
> In profuse strains of unpremeditated art.

The poem continues with stanza after magnificent stanza exalting the beauty of the skylark's song, spontaneity, grace, and freedom. Buried in the midst of the poem is a single stanza that is not about the skylark but about humans. In this stanza Shelley conveys in a few words not only the essential differences between the skylark and us but also much about the essence of humanity:

> We look before and after,
> And pine for what is not:
> Our sincerest laughter
> With some pain is fraught;
> Our sweetest songs are those that tell of saddest thought.

Life is not as good for the birds now as it was in Shelley's time, or in Jesus' time. Many beautiful species are threatened with extinction or have already become extinct. Jesus undoubtedly saw some birds that we will never see.

Pleasures can be fleeting; they need to be cared for. After each act of creation in the Genesis creation story, God said that it was good. It is our responsibility to see that God's creation continues to offer a sense of the pleasure God felt on the day of creation, and to pass that pleasure on to future generations.

THE MOST POPULAR PLEASURE

The number-one hobby of people in countries around the world is gardening. Something in human nature makes us fascinated with the soil, makes us love to plant, cultivate, and see something grow. A beauty is found in flowers and plants, both wild and cultivated, that is different from the human-made beauty of art or craft or music or poetry. When an artist crafts a painting or a sculpture, we perceive a direct connection between the hand of the artist and the created work. But when a garden comes into bloom, the connection between the gardener and the garden remains indirect. In the Bible the Apostle Paul used a gardening metaphor to describe the Corinthian Church: "I planted, Apollos watered, but God gave the growth" (1 Cor. 3:6). While we normally look for the deeper meaning of a biblical metaphor, here I want to take the metaphor in the opposite direction. In that space between the gardener's work and the growing garden, we see the hand of God.

Gardens require a bit of leisure time, both to cultivate and to observe. Gardens are rare in third world countries. Gardens require of their makers not only patience and industry but an economy that permits some leisure time. Such places tend to have the most numerous gardens, and the most beautiful ones. Japan and Great Britain come most readily to mind. The many days of slow and steady rain are doubtless a boon to the British in their gardening. On my first trip to Britain, I was struck by the fact that their flowers are simply bigger than ours. Rose gardens are everywhere, even in the smallest patch of dirt in front of the smallest apartment. The rose bushes are filled with enormous blossoms of beautiful color and tantalizing scent.

I have visited and enjoyed some of the most famous formal gardens in the world. Yet the ones that most stand out in my memory are neither the most famous nor the most carefully cultivated. More often they have been those slightly wild gardens in faraway places, where nature has been allowed much freedom. The skilled gardeners have subtly shaped nature rather than carved her out completely.

Two such gardens in faraway places took me completely by surprise. I did not even know they existed. The first was at Castle Dunvegan, on the northern end of the Isle of Skye, one of the western isles of Scotland. It is the farthest north I have ever been. The entire island is wild and breathtakingly beautiful. The gardens capture all that rugged beauty with many far-northern species that I had never seen and whose names I will never remember.

The second is nearly the farthest south I have ever been. It is Kirchener's garden in Egypt, on the banks of the Nile, near the High Aswan Dam. When I talk to my students about ancient Egypt, I tell them that it is a country eight hundred miles long and two miles wide. Except for the broader Nile River delta area, the population of Egypt to this day is heavily concentrated on the banks of the river. Beyond that narrow strip of fertile land lies nothing but miles and miles of desert on either side.

It was just before sunset, and we had far too little time. We were taken atop a hill with a spectacular view of the Nile, and walked through a gorgeous lotus garden with large deep green subtropical plants like I had never seen. A British diplomat originally created the garden in the nineteenth century.

I long to see both these places again, even though I know that, as with most such experiences, they will probably not seem as beautiful to me the second time. Fortunately, I have had the privilege of spending two recent summers on Roanoke Island, in the North Carolina Outer Banks, with its lovely Elizabethan Gardens. These gardens, too, have that carefully cultivated wildness that combines so well the crafted and the natural, the human and the divine. I have walked through them many times, never losing a sense of wonder at their beauty and a sense of peace that God, humanity, and nature can indeed be in harmony.

The Gospels do not indicate that Jesus was ever a gardener. He lived in what would now be called a third world country, where people oppressed by a foreign occupying army had little leisure and worked hard just to subsist. We can surmise, though, that Jesus did find pleasure in the flowers, and saw the wonder in the work of God in nature: "Consider the lilies of the field, how they grow; they neither toil nor spin, yet I tell you, even Solomon in all his glory was not clothed like one of these" (Matt. 6:28–29).

In those few words, Jesus captured a wealth of ideas. Solomon was the greatest and wealthiest king in all of Israel's history. His garments were the finest woven, the most perfectly fitted and sewn, the most beautifully dyed. Of all of Israel's kings, Solomon had the greatest sense of royal splendor. Jesus does not criticize the impressive beauty of all things associated with King

Solomon, nor the vast amounts of money Solomon had to spend to acquire those things. Jesus merely makes the comparison. The wild lilies of the field, those effortless creations of God, hold a beauty all their own. It is the simple beauty of white against color, of light against shade, of shapely forms with gentle curves that softly rustle in the breeze.

Most of us who read these words of Jesus' will never see lilies in the fields of Galilee, but we can all picture them in our minds. We know the simple beauty of a flower. For some of us, flowers are a passion. For others they are but a small pleasantry. Jesus knew that they were a part of the good life.

Jesus understood that the good life was not based on vast material wealth. To be sure, material wealth can bring us the leisure to enjoy the pleasures of the good life. Material wealth can even allow us to take some aspects of the good life to a finer level. It can bring us a nicer home, better food, finer wine, wider travel, and greater education. But for all of these material aspects we associate with the good life, it strikes me that few of those who amass great wealth really enjoy the good life. Too many of them, like Solomon, do not know how. The work of amassing the wealth becomes the all-consuming *raison d'être.* The pleasure the wealth can provide becomes secondary, if that.

Jesus knew the good life. He saw the beauty in the flowers. He experienced the joy of a wedding feast. He knew the love on the face of a child. He did not need a lot of money in order to live the good life. Neither do we. We need but a small space of land, some decent soil, a few seeds or plants, a little time and a little faith, and we can plant a garden. When our little space of beauty blooms, we know the good life.

THE PLEASURE THAT MAKES A CIVILIZATION

Historians have traditionally defined literacy as the difference between a culture and a civilization. The creation of writing by the Sumerians around 3000 B.C.E., and by the Egyptians within another century, made it possible for people to preserve permanent records of everything in their culture: lists of their kings and queens and their dynastic relationships; epics of their heroes, both mythological and historical; even the common, everyday transactions like the buying and selling of property and goods. It made possible the creation of the art of literature, the writing of poetry and prose, as things of beauty. These things make a civilization.

For many years scholars thought that preliterate cultures preserved the accounts of their own history quite accurately by retelling and passing down through the generations the stories of their history. They cited illiterate Bedouin Arabs who can recite the entire Qur'an from memory as evidence of the accuracy of the oral tradition. The problem with this is that the Qur'an is a fixed written text that is being memorized. Transmitting it through the spoken word over generations is not the same as oral transmission of stories and traditions that have never been written down. Testing the accuracy of these latter oral histories is extremely difficult because there are no written records with which to substantiate their accuracy.

Some remarkable studies were done in the mid-twentieth century on famous eastern European bards. Recordings made of fathers and mothers telling lengthy national and tribal stories were followed up with recordings of the same individuals telling the same stories fifteen years later, and in some cases, of their children telling the same stories twenty years after that. The studies showed that oral tradition did not preserve these stories nearly as accurately as we had thought they did. The storytellers were not merely passing on the traditions; they were also adapting and creating, adding and subtracting, and rearranging the material they had received.

Writing changes all that. Once something is written down and that writing is preserved, we have an accurate record of what the writer was thinking at the time he or she wrote, especially if we still have the original manuscript, or autograph, of the writer. With ancient literature, we rarely have original manuscripts. We have only copies of copies of copies, often centuries away from the autograph. In such copies of manuscripts, changes inevitably come into the text as it is copied and recopied. Most of the changes are simply copy errors; some are intentionally made by the copyist. Some of these changes are of a minor and innocent sort. For example, we find that Paul's Letter to the Romans was not written entirely by Paul. In Romans 16:22, we read, "I Tertius, the writer of this letter, greet you in the Lord." This otherwise unknown Tertius was most likely functioning as Paul's secretary, transcribing Paul's words into writing, but in this one brief instance, adding some words of his own.

Sometimes additions made to texts are less innocent. For example, all of the earliest manuscripts we have of the Gospel of Mark (we do not have the autograph of Mark or any other book of the Bible) end at Mark 16:8, without any resurrection appearances of Jesus. The women go to the empty tomb, and are told by a mysterious young man dressed in white that Jesus is risen and is going on before them into Galilee, where they will see him. Mark ends with the women fleeing the tomb in fear and telling no one.

This original Markan ending apparently did not satisfy later copyists. By the sixth century, manuscripts containing the Gospel of Mark began to have new endings with resurrection appearances, some of which were borrowed from the other Gospels, some of which were new. These new additions, and one in particular, have been a cause of consternation in the twentieth century because of Christian groups that have based their beliefs and practices on a literalistic interpretation of these verses. The chief verse in question is Mark 16:18, in which Jesus supposedly instructs all who believe in him, "they will pick up snakes in their hands, and if they drink any deadly thing, it will not hurt them." The snake-handling cults in rural Appalachia developed directly from this verse, which does not go back to Jesus or even to the original Gospel of Mark. All this is to say that even written tradition can be inaccurate. Oral tradition is even more inaccurate.

Unfortunately, we have no writings from Jesus. Not only are there no autographs and no copies, the simple fact is that Jesus, insofar as we know and insofar as the Gospels tell us, never wrote anything. All we have are his oral sayings preserved for a generation and then written down by the Gospel writers or their sources. Yet the fact that we have several Gospels that can be critically compared makes clear the essential accuracy of a substantial body of the teachings of Jesus.

We do not know why Jesus never wrote a book. Some scholars think that he, like the overwhelming majority of the people of his time, was illiterate. The Gospels show otherwise. In Luke 4:16–20, Jesus reads from the scroll of the prophets in the synagogue in Nazareth. Moreover, Jesus' knowledge of the Hebrew Scriptures and ability to paraphrase and quote them in arguments with the Pharisees is a good indication that he knew how to read them. That he was frequently called rabbi in the Gospels is another indication of his likely literacy.

Although Jesus never talks about the act of reading scriptures, the Gospels imply that reading them was a joy to him. His reading and interpreting of them—in many cases interpretations that were quite different from the traditional interpretations of the Pharisees—brought a new understanding of their faith to the crowds to whom he spoke. Jesus saw the love of God in the Hebrew Scriptures that he read and used. He did not dwell on the many texts that show the vengeance and wrath of God. He read with good purpose.

Although Jesus could read, he did not have much to read. Neither did anyone else among the Galilean Jews of his socioeconomic class. It is doubtful that Jesus had much else to read besides the Hebrew Scriptures. The printing press would not be invented for another fourteen hundred years. Books were scarce, and magazines and newspapers were nonexistent. Jesus never specifically instructed his followers to be readers. After his crucifixion and resurrection, however, everything changed.

The nascent Christian faith managed to survive for twenty years in an oral wilderness, until the Apostle Paul began to put its theology into writing. Less than a generation later, the words and deeds of Jesus were committed to writing in the Gospels. The new faith was giving birth to its own sacred scriptures. From that point forward, the Christian Church found its basis in reading and writing. No other religion has even come close to producing the quantity of literature that Christianity has produced.

It is fair to say that the Christians invented the book. To be sure, there were extensive writings called books before Christianity, but they were always created and copied in the form of scrolls. As far as we know, the early Christians were the first to cut papyrus or parchment into sheets, fold them in the middle, write on both sides of the page, sew the pages together in quires, and bind the quires together into books. All our earliest examples of the book form are early Christian writings, most of which are now included in the New Testament.

The early Christians could not get enough of books. They wrote, copied, and read far more than any other group in Greco-Roman society. They promoted literacy among their converts. Even though the vast majority of Christians, like the vast majority of people in antiquity, were illiterate, Christians from earliest times read books aloud, often in worship services, to the illiterate. The Jews had done this before them, and Jesus had done it himself at the synagogue in Nazareth (and doubtless other places as well). But the Christians did it to a far greater extent than anyone before them. Jesus knew the pleasure of reading. His early followers essentially created the pleasure that would come from books.

There had been book collectors, or more accurately, scroll collectors, before the early Christians. In the first century B.C.E., the writer, lawyer, and politician Cicero even had his own publisher, a man named Atticus. The library at Alexandria sought to acquire a copy of every book that had ever been written, a goal that was possible in antiquity, but no longer. During the first three centuries of Christianity, Jesus' followers did not have the privilege of having their own libraries or even their own church buildings, but they kept on writing, copying, and reading. When the emperor Constantine, in 313 C.E., declared Christianity to be a legal religion in the Roman Empire, there was an even bigger explosion of Christian literature. During the next century and a half, great Christian theologians emerged: St. Augustine in the Latin-speaking West, and the Cappadocians (Gregory of Nyssa, Basil of Caesarea, Gregory of Nazianzos, and Macrina) in the Greek-speaking East.

Civilization is fragile. It is easier to destroy than to create. Over the course of the fifth century, the Roman Empire in the West fell to illiterate invading tribes from the north and east: the Goths, Visigoths, Ostrogoths, Vandals, and Huns. Though learning and literacy would continue in the Greek-speaking Christian Byzantine Empire in the East, it, too, would see decline. By the end of the sixth century, the West had become almost entirely illiterate. For the next five hundred years, virtually the only people who could read and write were Christian monks. These monks helped preserve what little was left of the classical civilization of the West. Classical philosophy was largely preserved by the Muslim philosophers of the Arab world. This period was rightly known as the Dark Ages.

Around the year 1100, a revived European civilization began to emerge. Magnificent Gothic cathedrals began to spring up all over Europe. Whole towns and villages would be built around a cathedral. Gothic cathedrals were not only monuments to new architecture, with their massive vaulted ceilings pointing ever upward to God, they also promoted and housed the arts. Stained glass, sculpture, and fresco painting would take art to new heights over the next few centuries. The cathedral of Chartres, near Paris, is the greatest example, but many other cathedrals would be built or rebuilt during this period known as the High Middle Ages.

Literature, philosophy, and theology reemerged as well. The recovery of books of Greek philosophy from the Byzantine Christians and the Arabs in the Near East led to what the eighteenth-century historian Jakob Burckhardt would describe as the renaissance of civilization in Italy. The Renaissance would spread to northern Europe in the fifteenth century.

Through it all, the Christian creation and preservation of the book enabled civilization to survive. Thomas Cahill, in his book *How the Irish Saved Civilization,* talks about the monks on the remote and rugged island of Skellig Michael, off the southwest coast of Ireland, one of the most remote places in the then-known world. By the end of the sixth century, they were practically the only literate people left in Europe. They and subsequently their missionaries to other remote British islands such as Iona and Lindisfarne would create beautifully illuminated Bibles that both kept the word alive and created new art.

When Johannes Gutenberg invented the printing press in the latter half of the fifteenth century, the first book he printed was the Bible. The printing press would represent in many ways the ultimate triumph of the creative forces of civilization over the destructive forces of barbarism. Printing ensured the nonextinction of good books.

Printing also ensured the widespread dissemination of new and sometimes dangerous ideas. Martin Luther made expansive use of it to dispute abusive practices of the Catholic Church, disputes that soon led to the

Protestant Reformation. Two centuries later, Enlightenment philosophers used printing to spread the ancient Greek ideal of democracy on a new scale. The American, French, and other European revolutions against monarchical tyranny would result.

Printing also made possible a new love of the pleasure of books. Because books could now be produced on a scale previously inconceivable, they would be purchased and read in much larger numbers. There arose people who enjoyed the pleasure not only of reading but also of owning and rereading books. Undoubtedly this is a pleasure that Jesus would have partaken of and enjoyed, had it been available to him. The availability of books ushered in book lovers, bookworms, or bibliophiles, as we sometimes call them. Their personal libraries have not only enriched their own lives, but in most cases, have been passed down to enrich the lives of others.

Although I could not tell you who the first modern bibliophile was, the earliest personal library of significance that I have personally seen is that of the late eighteenth- and early nineteenth-century Scottish romantic writer Sir Walter Scott. Located in his home, called Abbotsford, in the Scottish lowlands, it is a magnificent personal library of a wealthy man, who learned so much from the books he owned and read that he was able to create the great literary panoramas of his heroic novels *Rob Roy, Ivanhoe,* and others.

Since Sir Walter Scott's time, two major developments in the collecting of books have helped expand the pleasure of reading. First, a wealthy businessman named Andrew Carnegie developed and funded the idea of public libraries. Public libraries are now found in nearly every little hamlet in the United States, and have made thousands of books available for all, rich and poor, to read. Second, bibliophiles of all sorts have created many highly specialized personal libraries. These libraries not only helped their owners to become experts in their fields, but they have also been passed on to other persons or institutions that have continued to benefit from them.

The passion of one such bibliophile has had a clear impact on my life. Frank Baker, a British Methodist minister who was also becoming a scholar of the life of John Wesley, began to collect books and materials by or about John Wesley. Baker and his wife lived on the legendarily paltry salary that Methodist ministers in England make to this day (they do much better in America). After World War II, however, Baker found that he could purchase Wesley materials, including many eighteenth-century editions from Wesley's own time, for very small prices. During the next twenty years, Baker amassed the greatest private collection of Wesleyana in the world. He not only collected; he read. He not only read; he wrote. By the early 1960s, he had come to be considered the world's greatest Wesley scholar without a university position. Dean Robert Cushman of the Duke University Divinity School offered him a faculty position at Duke, with the understanding that he would bring his library with him and that it would remain at Duke.

In the following years, Baker's library, a vast collection built on a shoestring, enriched the lives of hundreds of students, including me. In the early 1970s, I had a summer job collating the first six editions of John Wesley's *Explanatory Notes on the New Testament* for what was then the Oxford Wesley Works Project. The six editions were all made during Wesley's lifetime (1703–1791), and under his control. Although my work was tedious, one thing that impressed me every single day that I worked on the project was that my desk was the only place in the world that contained all six editions of these important books, and it was Frank Baker's passion for books and learning that had made this unique circumstance possible.

COUNTERFEIT PLEASURES

A warning is in order regarding the "counterfeit" pleasures that might slip into our thinking about the good life. When I say counterfeit pleasures, I refer to actions and choices that seem on some level to be related to the pleasures we have discussed, but that in reality have destructive effects on the good life. Those who believe, for example, that they are taking legitimate pleasure in sexuality or wine by being promiscuous or constantly intoxicated have missed the point. Such misuse of our God-given avenues of pleasure is based in, and perpetuates, a lack of self-control. Indulging in such pseudo pleasures diminishes one's ability to function adequately in societal, family, and individual relationships. It leads to ill health, disease, and the potential for pain that far outweighs any real pleasure derived from the experience.

Related to this is the fact that evil *does* exist in the world. Some Christians choose to blame evil on supernatural entities such as Satan, but virtually all evil is humanly conceived. Evil acts occur in every sector of society, among those who are poor and disadvantaged and in corporate boardrooms. My observation of those who carry out evil acts leads me to the opinion that the greatest pleasure, love, is unknown to them. Despite appearances to the contrary, I cannot believe that such people are at all happy. They hold themselves and others in contempt, just as do those who revel in counterfeit pleasures that deprive us of truly experiencing the good life.

We already know that evil is more than a moral challenge—it is a sociological challenge as well. Perhaps we will one day discover psychological and physiological routes for dealing with the problem of evil, just as we have developed chemical treatments for conditions such as schizophrenia. If we do, I hope we will recognize that God is working with us, through the pleasure of learning and discovery, to take something negative and turn it into a positive. God did that very thing through the death of a particular human being named Jesus, and God can do it through each of us as we strive to live the good life.

THE GOOD LIFE FOR JESUS

God has blessed the world with a vast number of pleasures. We all have the opportunity to embrace the good life. Jesus lived the good life; the Gospels give us a glimpse of what the good life was for Jesus. We have discussed most of the elements of his good life, and none of these elements required spending money. His good life was not tied up in owning things or controlling people. But he did have a good life, a very good life, up until those fateful days of his last week on earth.

Jesus appears to have enjoyed good health. Although he must have suffered the usual childhood diseases or caught a cold now and then, the Gospels give no indication that he ever went through a serious illness, had a life-threatening injury, or suffered any chronic pain. Jesus had the pleasure prerequisite, good health.

Jesus had a good place to live. Unlike the majority of people in his time, who never moved more than a mile or two from the place where they grew up, Jesus chose to leave the little village of Nazareth and live elsewhere. He chose to live on the northern shores of the Sea of Galilee, one of the most beautiful places I have ever seen. He made trips to the holy city of Jerusalem for the major Jewish religious festivals, but he did not choose to live there. The Gospels do not tell us why. It would seem that as a religious leader among the Jewish people, it would have been better for him to have lived in Judaism's religious center. For whatever reason, he simply did not feel at home there. Perhaps it was because of the tight priestly control over religious life there. Perhaps it was because of the stronger and more oppressive presence of occupying Roman military forces in Jerusalem. Or perhaps it was simply the natural, lush green beauty of the Galilean hillsides in comparison to the rocky barrenness of Jerusalem. For whatever reason, Jesus found a place to live that gave him great pleasure.

Jesus found good friends with whom he could share his love. These friends were both male and female. They were all Jewish, but they came from various strata of Jewish society. He got to know them well, and was able to spend much time with them.

Jesus found meaningful work. He left his adolescent trade of carpentry (or stone masonry), followed the lead of God, and crafted together his own new profession, one we might call ministry. It consisted of teaching and preaching the sacred scriptures of his religion, of healing the sick, and of speaking a prophetic word.

These were the principal pleasures of Jesus. There are a number of the basic pleasures in life that were not important to him or that he did not engage in at all. Most obvious are marriage and family. Although I think it is possible, perhaps probable, that Jesus would have married and had children if he had lived longer, he chose not to marry during his lifetime, even though at age thirty-three, he was quite old enough to marry.

Jesus also had relatively little connection with his own family. Though the Gospels give some indication that he remained close to his mother throughout his life, he does not appear to have had a close relationship with Joseph, who disappears from the New Testament after Jesus turns twelve. Likewise Jesus seems to have had little relationship with his brothers and sisters. His four brothers, James, Joses, Judas, and Simon, are named in Mark 6:3 and Matthew 13:55, but the Gospels contain no stories of any interactions between Jesus and them. The Gospels also indicate that Jesus had sisters, though none are mentioned by name and we do not even know how many there were. Jesus had numerous close women friends, including Mary Magdalene, Mary and Martha of Bethany, and Joanna, but he apparently did not have close relationships with his sisters.

Although tastes in food vary from person to person and culture to culture, everyone finds pleasure in eating. The Gospels have little to say about Jesus' pleasure in eating. As a male in a culture in which virtually all food preparation was done by women, Jesus appears never to have known the pleasure of cooking. Because he always lived with friends and never had a home of his own, he did not know of other domestic pleasures, such as gardening and home improvement.

Entertainment in antiquity, indeed up until the twentieth century, was generally homemade. People would sing, play musical instruments, tell stories, even enact plays. Books were scarce, and the ability to read them even scarcer, but at least there were copies of the Torah and the prophets in the synagogue at Capernaum for Jesus to read. Entertainment in an area like the Sea of

Galilee originated locally. The few traveling entertainers that existed then could make a living by going to the big cities, but they hardly ever went to rural villages in areas like the Galilee. Jesus enjoyed the few entertainments that were available to him, as the story of the wedding feast at Cana indicates. Jesus also provided entertainment with his teaching.

Jesus enjoyed the good life that was available to him. He made a good life for himself in the Galilee. One of the most important elements of his good life was that he strived to offer the good life to others. He did all within his considerable power to do so. His teachings and his healings improved the lives of the people who lived around the Sea of Galilee and in other places he visited. He found that his own good life was best when he did good for others.

9 / JESUS AND OUR PLEASURES

The simple pleasures that Jesus knew are still available to us today, although often in more complex forms. Daily life changed relatively little in the first eighteen centuries after Jesus' life on earth. Even the industrial revolution of the nineteenth century did little to change the essential pleasures of life.

My father, born in 1913, grew up in the rural agrarian South without electricity or running water. In his youth, railroads were a source of pleasure owing to the opportunity they afforded for travel, but my father rarely had a chance to ride on one. Automobiles were scarce and unreliable, and horses and donkeys still pulled carts and plows. Industrial machinery was limited largely to the big factories in large cities. The majority of people still produced most of the food they ate. Infectious diseases were still the major cause of death. Infant mortality was high, and life expectancy was considerably shorter than it is today. The principal operation that surgeons learned was amputation. The aspirin was the only pill that had been invented, but my father in his youth rarely saw one.

The pleasures that my parents knew were essentially those of the time of Jesus. In this way they were closer to him than we are today. Both my parents are still very much alive, and their generation has seen more change than any other generation in history, far more than mine or my children's.

Our world is flooded with a host of new pleasures that were unavailable or available only to the rich in earlier years. Many of these things, when they were invented, were considered to be pleasures, but are now considered to be necessities. Air conditioning, for example, has changed the face of the American Sunbelt. The summer heat of the American South and Southwest rendered these areas uninhabitable—at least as far as people who had grown up in other parts of the country were concerned. Air conditioning changed all that, and brought about a major shift in population. I grew up without air conditioning, but could scarcely think of being without it now. We did have refrigeration and central heat when I was growing up, but we lacked a dishwasher, garbage disposal, clothes dryer, microwave, and television. There were no fast-food restaurants; there were few restaurants of any sort. Traveling was hampered by bad roads, unreliable cars, infrequent motels with tiny rooms and large bugs, and infrequent restaurants with bad food and worse service.

Our pleasures are much more bountiful now, from choice of cuisine to travel accommodations to the everyday stuff of domestic life. A host of extravagant pleasures are also available to me if I am willing and able to spend the money for them.

In the complexity of twenty-first-century life, we deal with not only a new abundance of pleasures but a new set of ethical questions in our experience of these pleasures. Our new pleasures can also cause us to overlook some of those simpler pleasures that human beings have shared throughout history, pleasures that Jesus knew and enjoyed.

THE PLEASURE OF GOOD CONVERSATION

I have read that our closest relative in the animal kingdom, the chimpanzee, has DNA that is 98 percent identical to that of humans. Despite being so closely matched, however, they cannot share with us one of humanity's greatest and simplest pleasures—interactive speech. Jesus delved deeply into the pleasure of conversation. Today we have reason to think that this basic and beautiful pleasure is being diminished.

The Gospels have only the barest kernels of Jesus' conversations. They do not begin to tell us everything. The Gospel of John ends with the statement,

"There are also many other things that Jesus did; if every one of them were written down, I suppose that the world itself could not contain the books that would be written" (21:25). Although John's statement is hyperbolic, it does remind us of how little we have of the words and deeds of Jesus. We do, however, have enough of his words to grasp something of his character as a conversationalist.

Many of Jesus' conversations were adversarial. His most frequent opponents were the Pharisees, who were considered the best people of Jesus' time and place. They were the most devoutly religious, the most charitable, the most honest, and even the most loving of the people in Palestine. They had a positive reputation among their contemporaries. But because the Gospels almost always record Jesus in opposition to them, the Pharisees come across to us in a negative light. It is intriguing that Jesus seems to have singled them out as his chief opposition (or perhaps it was they who singled him out). In any case, Jesus chose to make his moral arguments against the most moral of people. He saw their weaknesses in a way that they could not. He spoke carefully and succinctly in his conversations with them. His criticism was often clever and biting, but always to the point:

> And as he sat at dinner in Levi's house, many tax collectors and sinners were also sitting with Jesus and his disciples—for there were many who followed him. When the scribes of the Pharisees saw that he was eating with sinners and tax collectors, they said to his disciples, "Why does he eat with tax collectors and sinners?" When Jesus heard this, he said to them, "Those who are well have no need of a physician, but those who are sick; I have come to call not the righteous but sinners" (Mark 2:15–17).

The actual conversation was probably longer than this, but Mark concisely shows the Pharisees' basic argument and Jesus' thought-provoking retort. To be with sinners is not a sin. Jesus knew that what sinners need is love, not condemnation. His medical metaphor must have made the Pharisees think, just as it provokes our thought today. His metaphor implicitly compares sin to a disease. Sin does not make us morally untouchable. Its symptoms may affect some people more than others, but it is not something to be shunned—it is something to be healed. Jesus was and is its healer.

Jesus had an ability to say a lot in a few words. This one retort speaks volumes, not only to the problem of sin and sinners but also to the character of the Pharisees. Our conversations today, especially the public conversations of elected officials and self-appointed experts and commentators, seem to convey less and less substance while the number of words increases by the ream and the tone becomes meaner and meaner. Jesus, too, could dish out stinging criticism:

> "Woe to you, scribes and Pharisees, hypocrites! For you tithe mint, dill, and cummin, and have neglected the weightier matters of the law: justice and mercy and faith. It is these you ought to have practiced without neglecting the others. You blind guides! You strain out a gnat but swallow a camel!" (Matt. 23:23–24).

Jesus perceived that, despite their basic goodness, the Pharisees had a major character flaw. They were righteous and they knew it, and they became self-righteous. Moreover, their righteousness was too focused on matters of less importance. Jesus names the weightier matters that the Pharisees at times neglect, "justice and mercy and faith," and then brings his point home with two brilliant metaphors. He calls the Pharisees "blind guides." Jesus' metaphor has become so familiar that we do not think about how brilliant it is. A guide is a leader. The Pharisees were considered the moral guides of the Palestinian Jewish people. Just as a "blind guide" is unable to effectively lead people, so the Pharisees were morally blind, and consequently unable to lead their people to the moral life.

Jesus then takes another metaphorical swing at the Pharisees by using hyperbole, a literary and rhetorical device that uses gross exaggeration for effect. The notion that the Pharisees would strain a tiny gnat from their food and yet swallow a camel is intentionally grotesque on a literal level. But Jesus effectively makes the point that the Pharisees' tendency to focus on minute points of law—for example, healing on the Sabbath—at the expense of larger issues—healing the sick—is a shortcoming in their understanding of God's law.

This type of argumentation may not be entirely pleasant or polite, but it is a far cry from the "insult fests" that pass for public discourse in recent years. Jesus' speech relies on the brilliance of metaphors to show the utter absurdity of a type of Pharisaic thought that Jesus believes does not promote God's Kingdom.

Jesus could also be gracious and kind in conversation. He could soothe as well as sting. We have seen this in Jesus' conversations with the woman at the well in Samaria (John, chapter 4) and with Mary and Martha of Bethany (Luke, chapter 10). His conversation with Zacchaeus the tax collector (Luke 19:1–10) is another example. Zacchaeus was the most unpopular man in the city of Jericho. Although the Bible rarely tells us much about an individual's physical appearance, Luke does tell us that Zacchaeus was very short. It seems as if virtually every culture has a bit of prejudice against the shorter members of society, especially short men. But it was not his size that made Zacchaeus unpopular—he collected taxes for the Roman government. Any Jew who worked for the Romans was unpopular among his people, but a Jew who collected taxes for their oppressors was especially hated. Even worse, Zacchaeus had become a *chief* tax collector. The Romans recognized that Zacchaeus was quite good at his job, and they rewarded him for it. Tax collectors commonly overcharged taxpayers and kept the surplus; this practice had made Zacchaeus rich. The Romans were quite willing to look the other way as long as they received their share. But Zacchaeus's own people despised him.

When Jesus came to Jericho, a crowd gathered. Curious Zacchaeus, eager to see who this new teacher was but too short to see him over the crowd, climbed up a sycamore tree. Jesus saw him there. Whether Jesus already knew who Zacchaeus was, or whether Jesus divined Zacchaeus's identity, we do not know. But Jesus called Zacchaeus by name: "Zacchaeus, hurry and come down; for I must stay at your house today" (Luke 19:5). Zacchaeus did as Jesus said. The crowd grumbled at Jesus' choice to waste a day with the most disgustingly sinful person in the city.

Luke reports very little of what was likely an extensive conversation. The end result was that Jesus persuaded Zacchaeus to change his life. Zacchaeus said to Jesus, "Look, half of my possessions, Lord, I will give to the poor; and if I have defrauded anyone of anything, I will pay back four times as much" (19:8). Jesus responded to Zacchaeus with words of comfort and explanation of his own mission: "Today salvation has come to this house, because he too is a son of Abraham. For the Son of Man came to seek out and to save the lost" (19:9–10).

As in his interactions with so many other people, Jesus cared nothing about Zacchaeus's social status or acceptability. Luke does not record Jesus telling Zacchaeus what he must do to change his life and gain salvation; Zacchaeus comes to that conclusion on his own. In fact, Jesus, in his conversations, rarely tells people what to do. Instead he leads them to come to their own conclusions. Those conclusions invariably turn out to be the right ones. When Zacchaeus states his realization that he must set his wrongs aright, Jesus takes him at his word, knowing that he is truly repentant. Jesus ends the conversation with the most comforting words Zacchaeus could ever want to hear. The salvation of God has come not only to Zacchaeus but also to his whole household. Zacchaeus, who had forsaken his people in pursuit of wealth, is again truly a "son of Abraham," one of God's own chosen people.

This brief story is theologically loaded. Our purpose here, however, is to look at Jesus as a conversationalist, and a couple of things stand out. Jesus does not condemn the sinner or the sin. He does not need to. Most of us already know our sins. Having someone else condemn them only makes us defensive. We need to be convinced that we can do something about our sins. We have to be persuaded that a better life awaits us—not only in the world to come but also in the here and now—if we leave behind our sinful ways and habits and turn toward a higher moral ground. We are rarely persuaded of this by someone else's words. We are far more often persuaded by someone else's example.

As I write these words, our country is in the midst of a series of scandals created by the boundless greed of corporate leaders who have illegally acquired vast wealth at the expense of their employees, their shareholders, the government, and the public. They are all Zacchaeuses, albeit at a higher financial level. Throughout the scandal, virtually all these leaders denied their moral guilt and sought loopholes, plea bargains, and hiding places for their wrongfully acquired fortunes. Through it all, I suspect that most will remain unrepentant.

There are always a few in such circumstances, however, who see the light of God's truth. There are a few who come down from the sycamore tree and have a conversation that leads them toward a new understanding of what they must do with their lives. An earlier scandal, Watergate, brought to the attention of the nation a rogue's gallery of unsavory characters. The one who struck me as the nastiest and most callous was Charles Colson. He was convicted and did his prison time. Prison was Colson's sycamore tree; from there he was led to see his wrong ways and what he must do to set things right. The prison ministries he began after his release are still going today. His work has changed the lives of many prisoners for the better. What Jesus did for Zacchaeus in an afternoon of conversation, he did for Charles Colson as well.

Jesus and Conversation Today

Can we as a culture once again know the pleasure of conversation? I think we can, although it may require that we swim against the currents of our time. Jesus offers us some help.

First, listen. Jesus listened. We do not have to dominate conversations with our own words and thoughts. We should do our best to discern what others are thinking as they are speaking, and respond to them without trying to manipulate their words to match an agenda of our own. What others have to say is important. We need genuinely to hear them.

Second, we should do our best to include everyone in a conversation. A duet when three people are present is no better than a monologue when two are present.

Third, we should speak caringly, not carefully. If we show genuine care for the other person or persons in the things we say and how we say them, conversation will become a pleasure. Even when we need to criticize, we can do so in a caring fashion.

Fourth, being right is not important. Good conversation is rarely a process of convincing or being convinced. Persuasion is the art of rhetoric, not the art of conversation. In conversation we seek not so much to change a viewpoint as to hear more viewpoints. It is acceptable for the other person not to think like you or agree with you.

Fifth, enjoy the pleasure. A good conversation, even if it is a heavy conversation on a sad topic or situation, will almost always end with a good wish and a smile. We know it has been a good conversation if we leave it feeling better than when we began it.

I recall one of the most memorable conversations I have ever had, one that manifested the principles of good conversation I have discerned from the Gospels. I should note that I have met and spoken a few words with a few famous people, including a former president of the United States, a former presidential candidate, a former prime minister of Great Britain, a former prime minister of Israel, and the queen of Jordan. Although I have never had a conversation of any length with anyone quite so famous, I did once have a lengthy and memorable conversation with someone who was famous at least to me and to my colleagues in the academic fields of religious studies and history.

The story of this memorable conversation begins with a phone call to my daughter, April, two years earlier, in the summer of 1992. She had just graduated from high school and been accepted by Yale University, where she would major in history. In this phone conversation, she told me that her academic advisor at Yale would be Jaroslav Pelikan, Sterling professor of history. I was speechless. Jaroslav Pelikan had been one of my intellectual heroes for decades. He is probably the greatest Church historian who has ever lived. He has studied in depth all the significant texts of Christian and Jewish history in the original languages. He speaks fluently all the modern European languages except Hungarian and Finnish. His reading is prodigious. He has a command of Western history and literature that few people in the history of the world could match.

I did my best to impress upon April how fortunate she was to have such a great man as her academic advisor, and how rare it is that great university scholars even serve as academic advisors to first-year undergraduates. After April entered Yale, I was always curious and delighted to hear about her classes and her meetings with Professor Pelikan. She told me about going to his house (which she said had many pelicans in its decorating scheme), meeting his wife, and spending a delightful Sunday afternoon in conversation with him and the rest of his small group of academic advisees. I was utterly envious.

In October 1994 I had the opportunity to spend several days at Yale with April. I enjoyed attending her classes and talking with her and her friends in her dorm room overlooking the sculpture garden of the Yale Museum of Art. The highlight, of course, was that April arranged for us to have lunch with Professor Pelikan. We joked about how I might embarrass her by fawning all over this hero of mine, or by being speechless in his awesome presence. I bristled somewhat when she assured me that he was just "a really nice old guy."

We met for lunch at Mory's, a legendary dining club at Yale. It was not crowded that day. The atmosphere was relaxed. I thought about how many wonderful conversations must have occurred there over the years.

Professor Pelikan insisted that I call him Jerry. I wanted to, and did, find out quite a lot about him and his life, but he focused the conversation on April and me. He had read my book about *The Shepherd of Hermas,* a turn-of-the-second-century Christian writing that did not quite make it into the New Testament. Our conversation revealed that I had learned from his insights, which was not a surprise, but that he had also learned things from me by way of my book. Given that very few people have read that book, this was, to be sure, a rewarding piece of news.

Our conversation ranged widely over topics of mutual interest. Jerry steered the conversation in a subtle way, and when I began to fall into the technical jargon of academic biblical studies and church history, he returned us to topics and language that were interesting to April as well. We talked, for example, about classical music, a passion that April and I share. One of Jerry's books, which I had not read at that point, is *Bach among the Theologians.* He explained to us the basic points of the book, how Bach's music, not just in its words but also in the very structure of the notes accentuated one theological concept after another.

After responding to my questions about his life and education, Jerry moved the conversation to April's abilities, interests, and potential directions she might take in life. I was amazed that he knew her so well. A professor who is famous and so busy rarely has the time to get to know his students so well. After lunch, April went to class. Jerry and I continued our conversation for a little while in his office.

I have seldom felt so good about a conversation; never have I felt so good about a conversation with someone whom I was meeting for the first time. Never during that lunch did I feel that it was a situation of my trying to "hold my own" intellectually with one of the world's great minds. His attention was focused only on us and the things we were all interested in. Never did he give any impression of being rushed or having anything more important that he needed to attend to.

I went away from the conversation not only stimulated, refreshed, and relaxed, but feeling that my life had been enriched. Unfortunately, American culture in this new century does not encourage this sort of conversation. Businesses and other workplaces press for more and more time on task from their employees. Quantity of work has superseded quality of life. Doors and cubicles separate us, and conference rooms are arranged and decorated in such a way as to never let a conference become a conversation.

Even in our colleges and universities, places where one would think that conversation would be particularly valued, less and less is done to encourage it. My own university has no faculty club or faculty dining room, not even a faculty lounge. The local restaurants are usually too crowded and too loud. On most days I bring my lunch, eat it in my office in five minutes, then get on to the next task. I am surrounded by wonderful people with whom to converse, but all too rarely do we find time for good conversation.

Time is the prerequisite for the pleasure of conversation. Friendship is both the producer and the product of conversation. Acquaintances become friends only when we take time to converse, and even then, only if we converse well. Jesus knew how to do it. He treated everyone he talked to as an equal, he listened, and he heard what others had to say and understood their points of view. He was slow to criticize, but when he did criticize, his criticism was right on target. In most cases it was criticism that genuinely helped those who heard it. Even in his most biting criticism, love was evident. Jesus knew the pleasure of good conversation. Almost all of us know it as well, at least on some scale. We can know it even better by following Jesus' example.

THE TRICKY PLEASURE OF POSSESSIONS

The Gospels tell of Jesus eating and drinking, seeing the beauty of nature, caring for people, and showing them the love of God. The Gospels never show Jesus spending money. They never mention a single thing that he owned. When he talked about possessions, more often than not what he had to say was negative. Three of the Gospels tell the same story of a rich young man who came to Jesus and asked him what he must do to gain eternal life (Matt. 19:16–30, Mark 10:17–31, Luke 18:18–30). Jesus told him to follow the commandments. The man replied that he had done all this since his youth. Jesus then told him one more thing he must do; it is one of those things Jesus said that we least like to hear. Jesus told the man, "Sell what you own, and give the money to the poor, and you will have treasure in heaven; then come, follow me" (Mark 10:21). The next verse is one of the saddest in the Gospels, "When he heard this, he was shocked and went away grieving, for he had many possessions."

We can rationalize this passage in many ways. We can say that Jesus spoke these words only to this one particular man, that he did not mean them for all of us. We might guess that this man was too attached to his possessions, too materialistic, and that even though he kept the commandments, his love of possessions was greater than his love of God. Perhaps the passage is not speaking to us because we are not rich. But such rationalizations fall short of exempting us from Jesus' words. Jesus speaks to us all through the Gospels, not just to the individual he is addressing. The story does not imply anything about the man's character or the quality of his love for God. And in the larger scheme of things, Americans are not poor; we are rich.

Jesus has other negative things to say about rich people. Read, for example, the story of Lazarus and the rich man (Luke 16:19–31). Consider also these words:

> "But woe to you who are rich,
> for you have received your consolation.
> Woe to you who are full now,
> for you will be hungry.
> Woe to you who are laughing now,
> for you will mourn and weep" (Luke 6:24–25).

Jesus' ministry was predominantly among the poor, the lowly, the social outcasts. In light of all this, it is difficult to legitimately rationalize our own acquisition of possessions and wealth.

Many of us would point to that one capitalistic parable, the parable of the talents (Matt. 25:14–30), and the almost identical parable of the pounds (Luke 19:11–27). The story of the talents is well known to most American Christians, far better known than Jesus' parables and sayings that put the rich in a negative light. In this parable, a man who is about to go on a long journey entrusts his property to his slaves. He gives one slave five talents, another two, another one, "to each according to his ability." A talent is a vast sum of money, perhaps equal, in Jesus' time, to fifteen years of a laborer's wages. We should remember that Jesus is telling a parable here, not a factual account. When the man returns, the slaves with the five talents and the two talents had used the money to make more money, each doubling the amount with which he had been entrusted. The slave who had received one talent had buried his talent in the ground so that he could return exactly what had been entrusted to him, for he feared the master's wrath would fall on him should he lose any of the money. On finding this out, the master says, "You ought to have invested my money with the bankers, and on my return I would have received what was my own with interest" (Matt. 25:27). The master then takes away the slave's one talent and gives it to the slave who had doubled his five talents. Jesus then remarks, "For to all those who have, more will be given, and they will have an abundance; but from those who have nothing, even what they have will be taken away" (25:29).

As with most of Jesus' parables, he does not tell us everything in this one. He leaves the interpretation to us. Is Jesus really talking about banking and investment, as a literal reading of this parable would indicate? Is he talking metaphorically about something else, perhaps the spiritual riches entrusted to each of us? If he is talking about wealth and investment, does this parable directly contradict his statements about the rich elsewhere in the Gospels?

None of these questions yield easy answers. Indeed, the one thing the parables tell us clearly is that Jesus did not mean to tell us everything clearly. The purpose of the parables is to challenge our thinking, to lead us to see things differently—not to spell out exact rules for us to live by.

Perhaps we would do best to understand Jesus' words on wealth and possessions as warnings to us. Our wealth is ultimately a trust from God, and wise use of that wealth will make more wealth, not just for ourselves but also for others. But profit margins and bottom lines are not in God's ledger; a better world is. Jesus enjoyed the pleasures of this life and sought to bring them to others, especially to the poor, the sick, and the outcast. The wealth that we have acquired is for our pleasure, but not for ours alone. As Jesus took genuine pleasure in the costly ointment that Mary of Bethany poured on his feet, so we may luxuriate in those pleasures that our lives afford us. Likewise, as Jesus fed the five thousand and healed the sick, so we should use the powers at our disposal, and especially the power of wealth, to feed the hungry and heal the sick throughout the world. Jesus sought to bring the pleasures of life to everyone. When we as individuals, as corporate businesses, and as a nation use our wealth for that same purpose, we follow in the steps of Jesus. If we use our wealth only for our own pleasure, we become those rich people whom the words of Jesus condemn.

But how tricky it all is. How much is enough? How much of what we have should go for others and for a better world? St. Francis of Assisi read the story of the rich young man, heeded the words of Jesus, and gave all he had to the poor. But we, like the rich young man, will not give it all away. If the words of Jesus truly speak to us, we, like the rich young man, should go away troubled. Jesus leaves it to us to resolve the problem of the trickiest pleasure. Like the slaves entrusted with the talents from their master, we will be held accountable for our solution.

THE PLEASURE OF GOING HOME

Life is hardest for the homeless. The millions who have no place to call home miss the pleasure that the rest of us consider a necessity, a roof over our heads. Though we consider it a necessity, for most of us, our home will be far and away our most expensive pleasure. Whether we own it or rent it, we will spend more money on our home than on anything else. If we have a mate, if we have a family, our home will be the focal point of our lives. At the end of the day, it is where we go to find comfort. It is where we will lay our heads for sleep. At the end of our lives, it is where we would like to die.

What is it that makes our homes so important to us? Is it something more than just the many hours that we spend there? For most, but not all, of us, our home is a haven, a place of relative peace in the midst of an increasingly chaotic world. Most of us go to work in the morning and return home late in the afternoon. When we cross that threshold, our bodies tend to relax. We slow down a bit. We look forward to an evening that will include food, companionship, and far fewer hassles than we have had to deal with at work.

This, of course, is not always the case. If there is conflict in the home, it can be a place of tension. For a single working mother, home can be a place of frantic work: trying to cook, clean, care for children, and get ready for the next day—she seems scarcely to have any time to herself. Others have to take work home, spending the hours between dinner and bedtime trying to catch up to where they or their bosses thought they should have been at the end of the workday. We all need to make at least a few moments for ourselves. When the children are put to bed and the dishes are washed, and the preparations for the next day are as far along as we are going to get them, we need a little time to sit with a glass of something and some relaxing music, to read a little in a book or a magazine, or perhaps to do nothing at all.

Jesus had virtually nothing to say about home life. This should not surprise us, for he never owned a home of his own and probably never even had a room of his own during the time he was growing up. When he said, "Foxes have holes, and the birds of the air have nests; but the Son of Man has nowhere to lay his head" (Matt. 8:20, Luke 9:58), he was probably referring to himself. He left his childhood home in Nazareth, and rarely returned. Mark tells a revealing story of Jesus' sometimes difficult relationship with his hometown:

> He left that place and came to his hometown, and his disciples followed him. On the sabbath he began to teach in the synagogue, and many who heard him were astounded. They said, "Where did this man get all this? What is this wisdom that has been given to him? What deeds of power are being done by his hands! Is not this the carpenter, the son of Mary and brother of James and Joses and Judas and Simon, and are not his sisters here with us?" And they took offense at him. Then Jesus said to them, "Prophets are not without honor, except in their hometown, and among their own kin, and in their own house." And he could do no deed of power there, except that he laid his hands on a few sick people and cured them. And he was amazed at their unbelief (6:1–6).

The Gospels make it clear, however, that Jesus frequently stayed in the homes of others. He spent more time at the family home of Peter in Capernaum, on the Sea of Galilee, than anywhere else. This house was excavated in the late 1980s, and can be seen today. When he went to Jerusalem, he stayed at the home of Mary, Martha, and Lazarus, in Bethany, which is just on the other side of the Mount of Olives from Jerusalem. At other times he stayed at the homes of Simon the Pharisee and Simon the tanner. Other people who are not mentioned in the Gospels likely took him in at various times as well. He was always appreciative of the hospitality. We cannot say whether he would eventually have had a home, had he lived longer, though that is certainly quite possible.

Despite his own lack of a home, Jesus would not have begrudged us the pleasures a home affords. Jesus would never have gotten his message out if he had not been able to rely on the hospitality of homeowners, and it is to the pleasure of giving such hospitality that Jesus calls us. Hospitality is as rewarding for the homeowner as it is helpful for the sojourner. The Letter to the

Hebrews puts it most poetically: "Do not neglect to show hospitality to strangers, for by doing that some have entertained angels without knowing it" (13:2).

THE PLEASURE OF FAITH

"Now faith is the assurance of things hoped for, the conviction of things not seen" (Heb. 11:1). There is no better definition of faith. The Christian belief in God is a conviction of something not seen. God is utterly intangible. God is not manifest to us through our five senses. Faith is a leap into the little-known. Faith is always subject to the rationalist retort: if you cannot perceive it through the senses or through scientific instruments, you cannot know that it exists. To the nonbeliever, any mental (Christians would say spiritual) perception of God is delusion. We cannot prove the rationalist wrong on this point. In John Updike's novel *Roger's Version,* a graduate student in theology with a graduate background in science seeks to prove the existence of God on the basis of probabilities in the formation of the physical universe. The theology professor who is the main character of the book is utterly unconvinced. We should remain unconvinced of such arguments as well. Proving the existence of God is not what we are about, for if we were to prove it, we would no longer have a need for faith. Certain knowledge removes the need for faith.

Faith, that conviction of things not seen, not even with microscopes or telescopes, is one of the pleasures of life. Of course, believers can understand and approach faith in numerous ways. For some, faith is a constant struggle with frequent lapses. The numbers of people who have lost their faith, particularly in our modern scientific age, are legion. Many consider faith to be public assent to a certain set of doctrines, a certain way of understanding God and Jesus. In many extremely conservative churches in America, for example, faith requires belief in a God who is about to destroy the world, but who will rapture out of it all the true Christians who have just the right beliefs, ultimately basing faith on the fear of eternal punishment.

With such current understandings of faith throughout the Christian world, it may seem strange to view faith as a pleasure. But Jesus shows us that God intends faith to be a pleasure: "If you have faith the size of a mustard seed, you will say to this mountain, 'Move from here to there,' and it will move; and nothing will be impossible for you" (Matt. 17:20). Biblical literalists have a lot of trouble with this saying of Jesus'. Try as they may, they are not able to move mountains. They can only conclude that their faith is inadequate, which is not the conclusion Jesus intended. In this passage, Jesus again uses hyperbole to bring home his point—he is not being literal. For all the miracles attributed to Jesus in the Gospels, never did he use his faith to move a mountain. Faith, Jesus is saying, even faith as tiny as a mustard seed, can make all sorts of things possible in our lives. There is pleasure in this wealth of possibility.

This book is written from the perspective of a person who has faith in Christ. But the book is not meant to define that faith. Faith can be as individual and different as the number of humans in God's creation. What follows, then, is but a mere sampling of the possibilities of the pleasure of faith.

As I write these words, I am listening to the music of medieval Gregorian chant, more specifically, the music of a remarkable woman we mentioned earlier, Hildegard von Bingen (1098–1179). A mystical writer who became a saint, Hildegard was also a composer. Her music is soft and restful, moves at a slow pace, and uses a minimum of instruments. The voices give the echoing sounds of songs in a cathedral. To my ear, though certainly not to everyone's, this music is more deeply spiritual than I ever thought music could be. One of my simplest and loveliest pleasures is to sit in my study, close my eyes, and listen. As I do, I have a sense that I am connecting with a woman from a thousand years ago who was closer to God than I will ever be. If I just close my eyes, her music focuses my attention on the presence of God. My body becomes relaxed. Peace prevails. No words are needed.

Although I know that I will have the luxury of this experience only for a few minutes—the cares of life and the demands of work will take me back—I do not feel rushed. There is no set of prayers I have to say, no people or situations I must remember to pray for. I simply sit and listen. When I am ready, I get up and go on to my work with a sense of peace that I did not have before. I have known the pleasure of faith.

A second example of the pleasure of faith is the sacrament of the Holy Eucharist, or Communion. I have the pleasure of being behind the altar rail as frequently as I am in front of it. When I am behind it, dispensing the elements to the people who come to kneel at the altar, I feel a bit like Hildegard. I am like a guide who leads people into the presence of God. Leading is easy; I simply say the words, "The body of Christ, given for you," or "The blood of Christ, which he shed for you." These words are two thousand years old, yet they still lead the person of faith to the same place. If I know the person's name, I will say it. I will look at each person and try to convey with my eyes something of the peace and love of God. On some faces I see the tears of a deeply felt spiritual moment. Others are at a place in their thoughts that I do not know or need to know. Many have no expression at all. I guide them with the words and with the elements I place in their hands or mouths. God then takes them where God will.

When I am on the laity side of the altar rail, my posture is one of receiving. I feel humble, kneeling in the presence of God, so complex, so boundless, so much more than I can ever know or understand. When I receive the elements, I experience Christ in me. I have no concern for defining that experience. Transubstantiation, real presence, memorial—these are all interesting theological concepts, but they mean little to me in that moment. The Eucharist surpasses all explanations of it. As I return to my pew to pray, I have the pleasure of Christ in me.

Faith holds limitless other pleasures. Giving and receiving the Eucharist are but two. Jesus softens the hand of God and touches us with warmth and comfort, his touch as gentle as a summer breeze. He gives us the pleasure of his presence, and affirms every other good pleasure we are blessed to receive.

THE PLEASURE OF HOPE

For the last six months, I have suffered from an often painful physical condition. St. Paul in 2 Corinthians 12:7 writes of his "thorn . . . in the flesh," and in Galatians 4:13–14, mentions a "physical infirmity" and "condition" that he suffers from. Scholars have often wondered what his physical problem was, for Paul never gives us even an inkling of a description of it. My guess is that it is one of those embarrassing chronic ailments that he would rather not describe in a public document. I won't describe my ailment either.

In the first two months that I suffered, I was often nearly paralyzed with fear. Though the condition is in no way life threatening, I feared that it would become so painful that I would not be able to stand it. My doctors thought the condition could be treated with certain drugs and would go away within a few weeks. Because the condition was not considered all that serious, I was not given serious narcotic painkillers. I was given only anti-inflammatory drugs, which seemed to do little or nothing to quell the pain. I would have some good days, as many as four in a row, when I thought I was getting better. . Then the pain would return with a seeming vengeance. At times fairly severe pain would slack off quickly for no discernible reason. At other times, when I was experiencing relief, the pain would come back quickly.

In dealing with the daily trials of my condition, I gradually learned a few things about it. I learned that the only things sure about it were the past and the present. I could only count on what had happened before and what I felt at this moment, for it might go much better or much worse very quickly. I also learned that there seems to be a point of maximum pain that it has not gone beyond. I can take that point of maximum pain. What was in many ways more difficult to take was the depression that came with the pain. My feelings about myself and about life in general seemed to be entirely controlled by the degree of pain I was feeling. Though I never became suicidal, I feared that if the pain got much worse, I might.

The turning point came on my worst night. The pain was so bad, and I was so upset, that I began smashing my hands against the walls of our kitchen and nearly screaming in anguish. Such behavior is utterly uncharacteristic for me. I could see that Marianne was upset. She told me that I had to do something about this very soon, the next day. I called my doctor, who prescribed new medication, and perhaps more important, an antianxiety drug. As the drug helped me deal with the depression and fear, it also seemed to help me deal with the pain. Better days came, and I started having more good days than bad. The doctors were convinced that the problem would soon go away altogether. At times I thought it would.

This chronic pain continues to come and go. Perhaps it always will. But I feel that I can now deal with it. Although I cannot quite control the pain, it no longer controls me. When I am having a bad day, I know there will be good days in the future. I treasure those good days, and retain hope that the condition will go away entirely. I can also hope that research will find better treatment of the condition, perhaps even a cure for it.

I have prayed much during these months; I have prayed for healing. Like most folks in such circumstances, I have prayed more and harder when the pain was most severe. I have also prayed for the people I know, and the millions I do not know, who are in far more severe pain than I am. One such person, the novelist Reynolds Price, wrote a book titled *A Whole New Life,* in which he tells the story of his own struggle through unrelenting severe pain that resulted from a rare and incurable form of cancer. Though he is now paralyzed from the waist down, Price learned to deal with his pain through training in biofeedback. Despite the limitations caused by his illness, he has gone on to be an even more productive writer. His writing about his pain has brought me the pleasure of hope and has helped me cope with my own pain.

I have thought and read about the problem of pain from a theological viewpoint. If God exists, is good, and has control over the entire universe, how can God allow massive suffering to go on in the world? Why, as so many have justifiably asked, do bad things happen to good people? I have no new answers to offer, nor any particularly insightful theological literature to which I might refer. I have no theological solution to the problem of pain.

I do believe that God created the universe. I believe that God, in ways beyond our definition or understanding, ultimately controls the universe. For whatever reason, God has set up the universe to run under principles that we call natural law, principles such as cause and effect and gravity. It may be possible for God to intervene in these principles, to make exceptions to them in exceptional circumstances, or even to change them, but God seldom does this. For the most part, we have to live within and be subject to the laws of nature. God entrusts to us the responsibility of working within nature to improve the human condition. Medicine and the other healing arts are a part of this. Through it all, God is somehow with us, in the very warp and woof of all that is or can be.

Concerning his own mysterious chronic ailment, Paul wrote, "Three times I appealed to the Lord about this, that it would leave me." In other words, three times Paul prayed for his own healing. "But [the Lord] said to me, 'My grace is sufficient for you'" (2 Cor. 12:8–9). It seems likely that Paul suffered from his ailment for the rest of his life. That may be the case with me as well. If it is, God's grace will be sufficient. The memory of the good days will help me get through the bad ones, and give me continual hope for more good ones. I also will continue to have hope for complete healing. Many people have been completely healed from ailments far worse than mine.

Hope is a mixture of memory and possibility. We know how things are or once were, and we can envision how things might be one day. In another letter, Paul said, "We also boast in our sufferings, knowing that suffering produces endurance, and endurance produces character, and character produces hope, and hope does not disappoint us, because God's love has been poured into our hearts through the Holy Spirit which has been given to us" (Rom. 5:3–5). Paul's statement is profoundly true at more than one level. All of us experience suffering in life. We hope for it to end. When it does end, perhaps even a long time after it ends, we can look back and see its value for us. We are stronger persons for having gone through it. We are persons of deeper character, better able to cope when suffering comes again. Looking back on that suffering, seeing our hope realized in the past, gives us hope that it will be realized again. Paul attributes that hope to God's love in our hearts through the Holy Spirit. I can think of no better attribution.

Hope is one of our few pleasures in times of deepest pain or need. At some point in our lives, we will move to the final hope. We know that death is certain, that one day we will be no more upon this earth. None of us knows what lies beyond. The Christian hope is that of a life beyond, a life that will be immeasurably and inconceivably greater than our life on earth. Some characteristics of that Christian hope are expressed, perhaps better than anywhere else, in the New Testament vision of the new heaven and the new earth, toward the end of the Book of Revelation:

> "See, the home of God is among mortals.
> He will dwell with them;
> they will be his peoples,
> and God himself will be with them;
> he will wipe every tear from their eyes.
> Death will be no more;
> mourning and crying and pain will be no more,
> for the first things have passed away" (21:3–4).

Almost all of us, even those who are in the midst of terminal illness, hold other hopes before that final one. Indeed those hopes are a chief motivator for living. We live because there are good things yet to come, and we have the pleasure to hope for them.

THE PLEASURE OF CHARITY

The King James Version of the Bible translated the Greek word *agape,* in the First Letter to the Corinthians, as *charity.* The well-known thirteenth and last verse of chapter 13 reads, "And now abideth faith, hope, charity, these three; but the greatest of these is charity." The English word *charity* has changed its meaning over the centuries since the King James translation was published. *Charity* no longer means "self-giving love." It has come to mean giving to persons or causes that need more than they are able to earn.

For many Christians, the first charity to which we give is the Church. Its work, which we consider to be the work of God on earth, is not the direct selling of a product or service. For all the variety of services that the Church may do for us and for others, it has only an offering plate, not a box office. Thousands of other charities have evolved, and we select causes that reflect our own cares and commitments. Our charitable giving is ultimately an act of *agape*; we give without expectation of tangible return.

Jesus had no money to give. He did, however, see the immense value of giving, as well as the pitfalls of self-righteous giving. The story known as "The Widow's Mite" is the best example of his thinking:

> [Jesus] sat down opposite the treasury [of the Jerusalem temple] and watched the crowd putting money into the treasury. Many rich people put in large sums. A poor widow came and put in two small copper coins, which are worth a penny. Then he called his disciples and said to them, "Truly I tell you, this poor widow has put in more than all those who are contributing to the treasury. For all of them have contributed out of their abundance; but she out of her poverty has put in everything she had, all she had to live on" (Mark 12:41–44).

This is another of those difficult stories of Jesus', one of those that perhaps we wish he had not said. When we face this story squarely, we see that Jesus' view is in many ways almost the opposite of our understanding in twenty-first-century America. We are exceedingly grateful for the charitable use of the wealth of the rich. We do not mind that their names are on buildings and on the charitable foundations they set up. Although Jesus does not speak specifically against the giving of the rich in this story, he does make it clear whose giving he values most highly. We, in contrast, think that rather than giving, the poor should be given to. We would be more likely to scold this poor widow for her terrible money management and warn her that she will never be able to pull herself out of her life of poverty unless she quits giving away the little she has.

What can we learn from this story? Three things come to mind. The first concerns those who are poor. Charity is a pleasure. For those who must receive it, it is a necessity for living. But those who receive charity should not be deprived of the pleasure of giving charity. In the years I served as a parish minister, I had relatively few poor people in my churches. One of the things that I noticed as I sat in the chancel when the offering plates were passed is that my poor church members almost always put something in the offering plate. I had the feeling that for them, even more than for my wealthier members, giving was a pleasure.

Second, we who give from our abundance should never think too highly of ourselves. We need to be thankful for the abundance from which we give, rather than take pride in what we have given. Our charity should be our personal pleasure, not our personal pride.

Third, we need to get over our habit of giving grudgingly. Paul wrote, "God loves a cheerful giver"(2 Cor. 9:7). When we have trouble being a cheerful giver, taking time to remember the extent of our own blessings is in order. By the good fortune of our birth in the most prosperous country the world has ever known, we have the opportunity to make a good living, a living that considerably surpasses our minimum needs. We have an abundance from which to give. That is something to be cheerful about.

CONCLUSION

We have touched on a few of the pleasures of life and what Jesus had to say about them. We have seen how Jesus enjoyed the pleasures that were available to him. Far more pleasures are available to us in our time than Jesus could have known. Although his time and place and context are far removed from our own, Jesus has some things to say to us about the pursuit of pleasure in the goodness of life. A number of those things have been examined over the course of this book. The Gospels contain a good many more.

We all have a tendency, when we read a text, to see what we are looking for. If we want to see a doom-and-gloom Jesus, we will. I am convinced, however, that if we read the Gospels as whole documents, if we try to take in entirety Jesus as he is portrayed, we will not find a prophet of doom and gloom or an ascetic prototype of a monk. We will find a man who loved life and loved other people more than anyone else ever has. We will find a man who not only enjoyed the pleasures of life for himself but who wanted to make the pleasures more readily available to everyone else.

It was the fear held by two small groups of people that cut his life short. The temple priests felt that he was a threat to their way of life, a way that had brought them considerable wealth, which came at least to some extent at the expense of the poor. The Roman occupying forces and their political leader Pontius Pilate felt threatened, wrongly as it turned out, that Jesus might lead some sort of uprising against Roman rule.

However we might understand the events that happened after Jesus' death, it is certain that many of his followers experienced the resurrection of his continued presence with them. Some of those followers would in the next generation write down many sayings and stories from his life. These writings, the Gospels, are our primary window into the life of Jesus. The invitation is for us to read them afresh, to read them as if we had never heard the stories before. The Jesus we will find in them may surprise us. He will surely please us. He will even show us the way to lives of greater pleasure than we have ever known.

ACKNOWLEDGMENTS

The idea for this book first came to me after working with one of my students, Jennifer L. Tenley, on a paper she presented to the Student Undergraduate Research Forum at Elon University in 1998. Jena's paper was a critical exegesis of Matthew 11:18-19, and its parallel in Luke 7:33-35, in which Jesus quotes his opponents as saying about him, "Look, a glutton and a drunkard." With my encouragement, she titled the paper "Jesus: A Glutton and a Drunkard," with a second subtitle that more clearly expressed the serious and scholarly nature of her research. The title drew a good crowd. The paper drew a good response. The idea of an anti-ascetic Jesus became firmly rooted in my mind. Jena is currently working on a master's degree in theological studies at the Candler School of Theology at Emory University, and plans to continue her work with a doctorate in religious studies.

I am grateful to Elon University for providing me sabbatical leave during the fall of 2001, when much of this book was written. As with any book, there is not enough space to thank all of the many people who played some role in its making. I am grateful to all my colleagues at Elon University, but especially three from the Religious Studies Department: Dr. James H. Pace, Dr. Rebecca Todd Peters, Dr. Jeffrey C. Pugh, and L. D. Russell. Their personal support has been invaluable.

According to a number of publications on universities in America, none has a greater degree of engagement between faculty and students than Elon. Over the years a number of students have found me as their mentor. Virtually all of these students have gone on to graduate work and pursuit of careers in some aspect of church or academic life, and all have had some influence on my career in general and on the writing of this book in particular. Nancy Thacker was the first, in the late 1980s, and William Walker, Wil Brown, Tom Newman, Malley Sumner, and Judy Drye followed in the early nineties. Then came Stacy Billman, Cathy Barker, Carol Creighton, Paul and Elysabeth Lyon, Kristen Harrison, and Jo Ann Barbour. The finest student mind I encountered throughout these years at Elon is that of Grayson Chad Snyder, who is now completing his doctorate at Syracuse University. Turning the millennium for me were Jena Tenley, Alex Wilson, Andrew Villwock, Nicole Scherle, Emily Schlaman, Bryan Stempka, Darice Fichter, Alison Lacek, and Ben Moore, all of whom are now or soon will be in graduate programs at various universities around the country.

At present I have the joy of being mentor to five students. I have never had more protégés at one time, and never been so close to any group of students. The first four have been in all my Greek and upper level New Testament classes. They also have considerable musical talent. One of my finest moments came when they performed a song they had written about me. Since they were all female and all in my Greek class, I dubbed their group "The Greekie Chicks." The name stuck. They are superb students in the classroom and wonderful friends outside it. They are Cindy Briggs, Margaret Anne Fuller, Lori Sciabbarrasi, and Sara Shisler. A fifth, Patricia Rivenbark, was not a Greekie Chick only because of scheduling difficulties, but is also an excellent student and a wonderful friend.

Apart from university life, my involvement in a local church, Christ United Methodist in Greensboro, North Carolina, has occupied most of my time. I am particularly thankful to the members of the Seekers Class, whom I taught for eighteen years. Special thanks go to Dr. Karl Stonecipher for filling in for me on numerous Sundays when I was away, and for his and Lynne's friendship, and for the long term friendship of Laura Stroupe, Bob and Mary Greear, Richard and Nan Sipe, and Tom and Gloria Jordan. I am thankful also to the members of the Wine and Classical Music group, especially to Dr. Steve

South for all he has taught me about wine, all the care he has given me as my physician, and for his and Barb's friendship. I want to express deep thanks to the Reverend Susan Norman Vickers for both her leadership at Christ Church and for her serving as pastor to me.

Some longest term friends deserve deepest thanks, Larry and Diane Kimel, Gray and Kay Tuttle, Bob and Ruth Smith, and Nelson and Becky Green. For many years of long and joyous gourmet dinners and conversations at their house and ours I am thankful to Drayton and Jane Stott.

My family has been a source of joy and inspiration. Thanks to my parents, Woodrow and Kitty Wilson, for everything they did so very well in my life, to my brother Gerald for his inspiration of my intellect, to my brother Tom for giving me his knowledge of the workings of the Church, and to my sister Nancy for the good joy she brings, and to their spouses, Virginia, J. P., and Ruth. Our son John and daughter-in-law Jessica have well begun their quest for the good life, found so much of it in each other, and share so much of it with us. Our daughter April has been my closest confidant and the person I most admire, as she continually gives her immense skill and talent to the work of justice and peace.

While all the above deserve credit for what they have meant in my life, none of them deserve any blame for what is written in this book. The person who has meant most to this book is Michael Wilt, my editor at Augsburg Books. I am deeply thankful to Michael for, first, having recognized in the proposal I sent him in the summer of 2001 a book that needed to be written; second, for having guided that proposal through the rigorous editorial approval process; and finally for the immense amount of labor he poured out over every word in the manuscript. His work has made this a much better book.

The last person to thank is Marianne, to whom the book is dedicated. No one has given me greater pleasure in life in all its aspects. Together we have found and live the good life.